WORD
FOR ALL
SEASONS

WORD
FOR ALL
SEASONS

Preaching Through the Christian Year

MARIANO DI GANGI

BAKER BOOK HOUSE
Grand Rapids, Michigan 49506

Dedicated

to

R.B. Kuiper

John Murray

John Skilton

N.B. Stonehouse

Paul Woolley

Cornelius Van Til

and

Edward J. Young

whose teaching at
Westminster Theological Seminary
(1943 - 1946)
enriched my understanding of
the incarnate Word revealed in
the written Word of God

Contents

Prologue

What can the pastor of a small country church, or a struggling city parish, ever have in common with men such as Chrysostom, Calvin, Knox, Luther, Zwingli, Wesley, Whitfield, Maclaren, and Spurgeon? A commitment to communicate the gospel truth coupled with the desire to preach the Word of God and lead men to know the God of the Word.

Charles Simeon, whose evangelical ministry in the university center of Cambridge was used by God for the conversion and confirmation of many, expressed the goals of the preaching ministry as follows: to humble the sinner, exalt the Saviour, and promote holiness. We desperately need a revival of such preaching today. The discipling of the nations and the strengthening of disciples depends on effective preaching.

The disturbing fact, however, is that today, preaching is often dismissed as an unimportant and irrelevant exercise. Some regard it as a boring interlude between the more entertaining musical portions of the service. Others feel that proclamations from the pulpit should be discarded in favor of group discussion. They ask: isn't it the height of presumption for any preacher to declare an authoritative message in an age of participatory democracy, articulate dissent, and the absolute denial of all absolutes?

Except for criticism of obviously unchristian talk masquerading as a message from God, such resistance to biblical exposition and application reveals an unspiritual and worldly attitude.

Strangely enough, even some believers who claim to have had a deeper experience of the Spirit may show signs of restlessness when exposed to the ministry of the Word. They pursue the easy path of feeling, subjectivism, and mysticism in looking for immediate communion with God. Do we really honor the Spirit when we turn aside from the disciplined study of what He has already revealed in the inspired Word?

If we belong to the Good Shepherd's flock, we will love the sound of His voice. We will know that man doesn't live by bread alone but finds sustenance in the words that come from the mouth of the living God. Let us prize preaching, and insist that our pastors feed us in the green pastures of Holy Scripture.

The apostle Paul once urged a cautious young minister to preach the Word. Whatever his responsibilities in the area of public relations, social concern, personnel recruitment, pastoral counseling, and church administration, Timothy had to understand the primacy of preaching and was challenged to present the truth plainly in the power of the Spirit. What Paul urged Timothy to do we must encourage our ministers to achieve in the interests of fulfilling their ministry.

Far from depreciating preaching, we should learn to appreciate afresh the worth of a ministry devoted to the presentation of the incarnate Word from the written Word. Biblical preaching helps us to grow in the understanding of doctrine, duty, and destiny.

Old Testament believers were under sacred obligation to hand down the Lord's precepts and promises to their children (Deut. 6:1-9). Family teaching was supplemented by the public reading of the law of God every seven years, (Deut. 31:9-13). True religion revived in the reigns of Jehoshaphat and Josiah because divine revelation was recovered and proclaimed (II Chron. 15:3; 17:7-9; 35:3). Ezra and his associates both read and explained the inspired Scriptures so that no one would miss the message of God through His Word (Neh. 8:7, 8).

Sabbath gatherings in the synagogues featured the reading of the Scriptures, followed by an exposition of the same passages.

The true prophet in Israel was a spokesman for God. Of course, there were also false prophets, windbags who had been given nothing to say, but said it well. True prophets served as bearers of a message from the heart and mind of God. At times they showed foresight and uttered prophecies to be fulfilled in the future. On many occasions they demonstrated insight, a clear perception of the real issues, and demanded repentance and reformation in the lives of the people. Whether foretelling or telling forth, speaking to their contemporaries or looking ahead to the coming of the Messiah, they spoke at the direction of the Spirit of God. He guided them in their preaching as they pronounced judgment on sin and promised salvation through Christ.

In the New Testament, God continued to use preaching to communicate His truth. John the Baptist was essentially a prophet-preacher who prepared the way for Him who is the Way. John called men to repentance and faith. He was the voice crying in the moral and spiritual wilderness of the world. Then comes Jesus. How? Preaching!

Our Lord's announcement of the nearness of the kingdom of God was related to the necessity of repentance and belief in the gospel. This was the message He preached in synagogue and marketplace (Mark 1:14-15). The apostles engaged in preaching, far more than in healing or administration. They considered themselves to be heralds, messengers, spokesmen for God. As men authorized by the Lord and empowered by His Spirit, they preached, proclaimed, heralded, evangelized, taught, and transmitted the truth.

Their apostolic testimony, whether spoken or written, concentrated on the presentation of Jesus as the fulfillment of the messianic promises in the Old Testament Scriptures. Jesus was the answer to man's need. They declared what God had done in Jesus the Christ, who was anointed to be the prophet, priest, and king of His people. They proclaimed His birth, death, and resurrection. They made known His humiliation and exaltation. They presented His humanity and His deity. And they did all this with one goal in mind: the conviction, conversion, and confirmation of those who heard the Word (Acts 10:34-43; 13:16-41; 17:22-31).

The apostles were assisted in their preaching by deacons such as Stephen and Philip. These men focused on Jesus Christ, declaring the truth about Him in terms of Old Testament promise and New Testament fulfillment. The apostles provided for the transmission of the Christian message not only by their writings but also by arranging for the message to be handed down from one generation to the next by faithful servants of the Word (I Tim. 4:13-14; II Tim. 2:2, 15; 3:14-17; 4:1-5).

Apostolic preaching expounded the Scriptures and presented Christ in the power of the Spirit. Those New Testament preachers relied on His presence and power to render their preaching effective so as to further the gospel. They knew that the preaching of the cross would save sinners, without gimmickry or sensationalism, without show-business or sales techniques, because the Holy Spirit was at work as the Word was preached.

Paul was aware of this in the evangelization of Thessalonica. Reviewing the impact of the gospel message on that seaport city, he recalled how the gospel had come to them not simply with words, but also with power and with the Holy Spirit, who brought deep conviction to both the preachers and the hearers of the Word. Thus, the Thessalonians turned to God from idols. They began serving the living and true God, and looked forward to the return of His Son from heaven. Their lives were henceforth dedicated to Him who was raised from the dead and would rescue them from the wrath to come (I Thess. 1:4-10).

Concerning his preaching at Corinth, Paul recalled that he did not use mere eloquence or worldly wisdom, but proclaimed to the people of that corrupt city his testimony of God in the power of the Holy Spirit. He concentrated on Jesus Christ, especially on Him as crucified, sacrificed for sinners, and accomplishing atonement. His preaching was effective in bringing some to repentance and faith because it was accompanied by a demonstration of the Spirit's power. The faith of those who were thus converted rested not on the works of men but on the power of God (I Cor. 2:1-5).

We need to recover a sense of the importance of preaching. Real preaching. Preaching designed to present Jesus Christ as Saviour and Lord, on the basis of what is written in the Word. How shall people turn to Christ for salvation unless they believe in Him? And how can they believe in Him if they've never heard of Him? And how can they hear about Him unless someone preaches to them? Saving faith results from hearing the message, and the message is heard through the proclamation of Christ (Rom. 10:14-17).

The Reformation was characterized by the preaching of the Word of God. The Reformers studied, expounded, and applied biblical revelation with godly zeal. Luther, for example, regarded himself as one called to speak for God to man. Luther listed the ten virtues a preacher should have, as follows: first, he must be able to teach; second, he should have a good head; third, he must be articulate; fourth, he should have a good voice; fifth, a good memory; sixth, he should know how to stop; seventh, be industrious in his work; eighth, willing to hazard life and limb in his work; ninth, he should let himself be plagued by everybody; finally, he should patiently bear with the fact that nothing is more easily and quickly seen in preachers than their faults. He stressed that a preacher must know his Bible thoroughly and declare its truths plainly. On one occasion, Luther said: "I know for sure that my ministry is pleasing to the divine Majesty ... I know that on the last day, God will attest that I have preached rightly. If I were not sure of this so that in my heart I could build on it and depend on it, it would be much better for me to keep my mouth shut. But a preacher must have this confidence, that he is speaking not his own word but the Word of the Lord Jesus Christ. If we have Christ's Word and speak it, then we also have this confidence."[1] And "a Christian, whether he is a preacher or a hearer, must be sure that he is speaking and hearing, not his own word but God's Word; otherwise it would be better if he had never been born, and preacher and hearer together must go to the devil".[2]

Calvin not only commented extensively on the Scriptures but preached the Word constantly. His aim was always evangelical and moral, not speculative. He asked, "What is the design of the preaching of the Word, the sacraments, the holy assemblies, and the whole external government of the Church, but that we may be united to God?"[3]

Calvin was convinced that the teachings of a minister should be approved on the sole ground of his being able to show that what he says comes from God: "No man ought to be heard, unless he speak from the mouth of God." And "faithful teachers, who know well the nature of their calling, are fortified and armed by Him with an unshaken firmness, so that

1. *What Luther Says*, compiled by Ewald M. Plass, 3 vols. (St. Louis: Concordia Publishing House, 1959), no. 3551.

2. Ibid, no. 3552.

3. John Calvin, *Commentary on the Book of Psalms*, trans. James Anderson, 5 vols. (Edinburgh: Calvin Translation Society, 1845), I: 409, 410 (on Ps. 24:7).

under the guidance of God, they may boldly bid defiance to all mortals".[4]

The Reformers often presented a preaching series expounding and applying entire books of the Bible. They took seriously both the reality of biblical revelation, given by divine inspiration, and the necessity of hearing and obeying that Word in daily life. And so must we.

There has been a decline in the level of expository preaching marked by reverence for the God of the Word and relevance to the condition of the world. Why? Undoubtedly, the skeptical approach to Scripture advocated by theological liberalism has contributed to this deplorable decline. By denying the verbal inspiration of the Bible, doubting the authenticity of the prophetic-apostolic testimony, subjecting the Scriptures to a demythologizing process, looking at the Bible as valid only in those points where its teachings can be drawn on to support social theories currently in vogue, these religious humanists have contributed to the dilution of biblical authority and proven counter-productive to the practice of real preaching. The truth is that "Radical interpretations of the Bible have influenced preaching for evil".[5]

Even where an orthodox Scriptural doctrine is firmly professed and is compatible with the teaching of historic Christianity and the testimony of Scripture, preaching that is genuinely biblical may not always be heard. Biblical preaching demands far more than taking a text. Too many evangelicals do three things with a text: they take it, leave it, and never go back to it. The text becomes a pretext for the presentation of generalities or speculations which ignore the actual context and the practical purpose of the passage allegedly chosen for the sermon. In some churches the texts may vary but the same

---

4. Calvin, *Commentary on the Gospel According to John*, trans. William Pringle, 2 vols. (Edinburgh: Calvin Translation Society, 1847), I: 336 (on John 8:26).

5. Carl G. Kromminga, "preach, preaching," in *Baker's Dictionary of Theology*, ed. E.F. Harrison (Grand Rapids: Baker Book House, 1960) p. 415.

sermons keep being heard as certain topics run their course
and then are re-run with regularity. Trivialities may also be
allowed to displace the centrality of Jesus Christ.

It is high time that we start to match our preparation and
presentation of sermons with the high doctrine of biblical inspiration and authority that we profess. This will mean
rediscovering the wonder of interpreting the Scriptures in
terms of the person and work of Christ. It involves the
Christological interpretation of the Bible. We have sufficient
warrant to follow this approach in the practice of our Lord and
His apostles. The speeches contained in the Acts preserve the
message of the apostles. What was it? The interpretation of
the Old Testament in the light of the Christ whose story is told
in the New Testament. He was presented as the fulfillment of
God's promises and the answer to man's need. Our Lord encourages us to search the Scriptures because they testify of
Him (John 5:39). If we are looking for Christ, we will find Him
there. We come to know the incarnate Word through the written Word. Let us be led by the Spirit of Christ to see Him in
the Scriptures (Luke 24:25-27, 44-47).

One of the better ways to do this is to plan a year's pulpit
ministry with the framework of the Christian Year in mind.
Does the thought of such advance planning sound unspiritual?
Give it another thought.

Andrew W. Blackwood, who served as Professor of Homi-
letics at Princeton Theological Seminary for many years, encouraged me to plan pulpit ministry on a long-range basis. By
his books and his personal comments when he attended Philadelphia's Tenth Presbyterian Church during my pastorate
there, Dr. Blackwood stressed that "a wise minister preaches
according to a program...almost every strong pastoral
preacher has had some way of planning his pulpit work"[6].
There's nothing unspiritual about planning and preparing

6. Andrew W. Blackwood, *Planning a Year's Pulpit Ministry* (New York:
Abingdon-Cokesbury Press, 1942) p. 15.

prayerfully to feed the flock of God in the green pastures of the Word. Indeed, "Under the guidance of the Holy Spirit, the minister should be able to plan his pulpit work with practical wisdom, and then he should carry out his program with increasing joy".[7]

There is an antecedent for the Christian Year in the revelation of the Old Testament. In obedience to the commands of God, the Israelites observed several festivals throughout the year. They not only rested and worshipped on the Sabbath each week, but they celebrated God's mighty and merciful acts on such feasts as Passover, Unleavened Bread, Weeks, and Tabernacles. They kept the festivals of Purim and Hanukkah, and solemnly marked the Day of Atonement with fasting and sacrifice. "Jewish Christians continued observing the Jewish feasts, doubtless with a Christian meaning, but except for Passover and Pentecost they soon faded out".[8] In their place came commemorations of Christ's birth, death, resurrection, ascension, and outpouring of the Spirit.

The celebration of these events, year by year, reminds us of the truth that our faith is firmly rooted in the soil of history. We rely not on feelings but on facts, on what actually happened when God redeemed His people for all time in the person and work of Jesus Christ.

Preachers should welcome this framework of the Christian year for their pulpit ministry since it provides a safeguard against undue subjectivism in sermonizing and focuses attention on the great redemption wrought by the Son and applied by the Spirit, according to the Scriptures.

God has given us a Word for all seasons. Let us consider that Word: Christ with us, for us, over us, within us. Let us proclaim Him with freshness and faithfulness in all the changing scenes of life.

---

7. Ibid, p. 31.

8. H.L. Ellison, "feasts," in *Baker's Dictionary of Theology*, p. 217.

1

Christ With Us

Heralding His Incarnation

The Christ of Scripture is a living and loving Saviour. He is not static but dynamic. He came from heaven to earth in the fullness of time, and comes to us now through the word of the gospel, and shall come again at the end to judge the world in righteousness. It is this movement of Christ that we commemorate and celebrate in the Advent season.

Advent, of course, is derived from the Latin word "adventus", which is derived from the Greek term *epiphaneia*, transliterated as epiphany, which refers to the appearing of Christ in grace and His return in glory. During the weeks of Advent, we focus on the incarnation. Yet we ought not to lose sight of the fact that the Christ who came at Bethlehem draws near to us now as His Spirit speaks to us in the Scriptures. Nor should we forget that He shall some day come again to judge the quick and the dead.

19

PROMISE

The Old Testament is filled with prophetic promises of the Saviour's advent, designed to kindle and sustain the flame of faith in the hearts of people oppressed by the power of sin and confronted with the grim reality of death.

When Adam and Eve disobeyed God's command at the instigation of the seducer of souls, they lost paradise for themselves and the entire human race to come. Yet the holy God did not merely pronounce judgment upon the transgressors, but revealed His purpose of grace. He would not abandon the field to the foe. Intervening through a promised liberator, He would defeat the devil and restore what sin had ruined. God said to the serpent, satanic instrument of the temptation in Eden, "I will put enmity between thee and the woman, and between thy seed and her seed; it shall bruise thy head, and thou shalt bruise his heel" (Gen. 3:15).

In this protevangelium, God declares His intention to reclaim His lost creation through a Saviour born of woman. The Lord will save sinners by means of a man, not an angel. In the process of redemption, this liberator will be wounded by the enemy. But he will also crush the serpent's head in final victory.

As we trace the progressive revelation of God's gracious purpose to save, we learn that the deliverer will not only be born of woman but also descend from the line of Abraham. When the Lord summoned Abraham from Ur of the Chaldees, He gave him these wonderful promises: "I will make of thee a great nation, and I will bless thee, and make thy name great; and thou shalt be a blessing . . . and in thee shall all the families of the earth be blessed" (Gen. 12:2, 3). Through a descendant of Abraham would blessing come to the peoples of the world.

The deliverer, moreover, will come through the line of Isaac, rather than Ishmael; of Jacob, rather than Esau. And of Jacob's sons, Judah shall be the continuing link with the promised Messiah (Gen. 49:10). The prophecies become even more specific when they point to the house of David and a royal person who will be both the descendant and master of Israel's great king (II Sam. 7:13). The prophet Isaiah foretells Messiah's birth of a virgin, and then describes His character in these memorable words: "For unto us a child is born, unto us a son is given: and the government shall be upon his shoulder: and his name shall be called Wonderful, Counsellor, the mighty God, the everlasting Father, the Prince of Peace. Of the increase of his government and peace there shall be no end, upon the throne of David, and upon his kingdom, to order it, and to establish it with judgment and with justice from henceforth even for ever. The zeal of the Lord of hosts will perform this" (Isa. 9:6, 7).

The prophet Micah declared that the shepherd-king sent to liberate and bless shall be born not in Jerusalem but in Bethlehem: "But thou, Bethlehem Ephratah, though thou be little among the thousands of Judah, yet out of thee shall he come forth unto me that is to be ruler in Israel; whose goings forth have been from of old, to everlasting" (Mic. 5:2). How appropriate that the One who is the bread of God, the bread of life, the bread come down from heaven, should be born in Bethlehem — which means "the house of bread!"

This promised Saviour will be supremely qualified for His redemptive mission. He grows from the stock of Jesse and is a branch of David's family tree, but is endowed with the Spirit of the Lord to fulfil His incomparable calling. On Him shall rest the Spirit of wisdom and understanding, of counsel and power, of knowledge and the fear of the Lord. He shall not judge according to mere appearances nor come to decisions on the basis of hearsay, but judge the case of the poor with justice and defend the humble in the land with equity. By the might of His word shall He strike down the ruthless and slay the wicked. And the result of His righteous rule shall be abounding peace. In the messianic age, the kingdom shall be filled with the knowledge of the Lord as the waters fill the sea (Isa. 11:1-9).

Across the centuries, God sent His servants, the prophets, to bear His word of promise concerning the One who was to come. Then, "when the time had fully come, God sent his Son, born of a woman, born under law, to redeem those under law, that we might receive the full rights of sons" (Gal. 4:4, 5). The promise was kept as prophecy matured at last into history.

THE PROCESS

How did God send His beloved and unique Son into the world? On the basis of what the Bible says, we believe that Christ, the Son of God, became man, by taking to himself a true body and a reasonable soul, being conceived by the power of the Holy Ghost, in the womb of the Virgin Mary, and born of her, yet without sin".[1] This is plainly taught in Matthew 1:18-25, and Luke 1:26-35. "It is undeniable that His incarnation and virgin birth are intimately bound together in the historic faith of the Church".[2]

Yet there are those who definitely deviate from the historic faith of the gospel founded on the Holy Scriptures. One theologian remarks, "The question as to whether Jesus was born of a virgin is one on which the opinion of Christians differ, and the biblical accounts do not throw clear light upon it." Despite what Matthew and Luke so plainly present as historic reality, this author continues: "Jesus seems generally to have been regarded in Nazareth as Joseph's son. The letters of Paul and the Gospel of John, which throughout affirm the divinity of Christ, make no mention of the virgin birth. It does not appear in Mark, the earliest gospel. These facts lend support to the view that the story of a physical miracle in connection with Jesus' birth is part of the tradition that developed after the

1. Westminster Shorter Catechism (1647) in *The Creeds of Christendom*, compiled Philip Schaff, 3 vols. (New York: Harper & Brothers, 1877), Q. 22 (III:680).

2. F.F. Bruce, "The Person of Christ: Incarnation and Virgin Birth," in *Basic Christian Doctrines*, ed. Carl F.H. Henry (New York: Holt, Rinehart & Winston, 1962) p. 128.

early Christians had for other reasons become convinced of his divinity".[3]

The truth, nevertheless, is that both Matthew and Luke report the story of the supernatural conception and virgin birth of Jesus Christ as history. What if it does not occur in the narratives of Mark and John? How many times does God have to say something for it to be true? Is the virgin birth of Christ any more incredible than His resurrection from the dead on the third day after His crucifixion?

What if there is no explicit reference to the supernatural conception of Jesus in the letters of Paul? The fact that he doesn't mention the virgin birth doesn't prove that it was unknown to him. On the contrary, "the entire Christology of Paul is a powerful witness to the same event that is narrated in Matthew and Luke; the religion of Paul presupposes a Jesus who was conceived by the Holy Ghost and born of the Virgin Mary".[4] Once doubt and unbelief are allowed to begin obliterating parts of the biblical witness to Jesus Christ, where is the line to be drawn? We are not given license to pick and choose from some scriptural smorgasbord those aspects and elements of His story which are acceptable to our finite and sin-affected minds. We must believe all that the prophets and apostles tell us concerning Him.

Our very salvation depends upon it. Either the Son of God became man through the wonder of the incarnation and the virgin birth or we do not have a Mediator who has entered this world of time and space to save us from our sins. We must insist on the historical realities basic to saving faith. We have not followed myths, or legends, or "cleverly invented stories," but the testimony of credible witnesses who point to what actually happened (II Peter 1:16).

---

3. Georgia Harkness, *Understanding the Christian Faith* (Nashville: Abingdon-Cokesbury, 1947) p. 76.

4. J. Gresham Machen, *What is Christianity?* (Grand Rapids: Eerdmans, 1951) p. 76.

The Christian message comes to us through the Bible, which gives us an authentic, authoritative account of God's revelation. It tells us how sinners can be forgiven and restored to fellowship with the living God. The Bible reveals that God took the initiative, through his sovereign grace, to save us from the penalty and power of our sins. He demonstrated this in providing Jesus Christ to save sinners. This sending of the Son involves no theories or speculations but historical events, anticipated by prophetic promises and fulfilled by what actually happened. "For God so loved the world, that he gave his only begotten Son, that whosoever believeth in him should not perish, but have everlasting life" (John 3:16, KJV).

Christian experience confirms the gospel message. For example, we understand the truth of the atonement wrought by Christ, and discover Him to be a living Saviour today. But if Christ had not been conceived by the Holy Ghost and born of the virgin Mary, nor given Himself for us in sacrifice on the cross outside the walls of Jerusalem, we could have no valid personal experience of Him as our Redeemer. Christian experience depends on historical realities. It is fact that supports faith, not faith that creates the story.

At the beginning of the Christian era, "It was emphatically not a case of community creating the supernatural tradition, the Church producing the faith it lives by; the truth is the exact reverse. It was a case of supernatural facts creating the community, and doing it with such irresistible momentum that to this day the gates of Hell have not prevailed against it".[5]

Our salvation depends on certain events, on what really happened when Jesus came, lived, died, rose again, and ascended into heaven. Our spiritual life is related to the truth of the biblical record of the history of redemption. Receiving the record as true and trusting in the Christ it presents, we experience the forgiveness of sins and peace with God that are the essence of new life (John 20:31).

---

5. James S. Stewart, *A Faith to Proclaim* (London: Hodder & Stoughton, 1952) p. 26.

PERSON

We believe that Jesus Christ is a unique person. The eternal Son of God became man without ceasing to be God's equal. He is now both "God and man, in two distinct natures, and one person forever".[6]

The classic definition of the two natures in the one person of Jesus Christ was developed by the Council at Chalcedon in 451. That Council declared, "We ... teach men to confess one and the same Son, our Lord Jesus Christ, the same perfect in Godhead and also perfect in manhood; truly God and truly man, of a reasonable (rational) soul and body; consubstantial (essential) with the Father according to the Godhead, and consubstantial with us according to the Manhood; in all things like unto us, without sin; begotten before all ages by the Father, according to the Godhead, and in these latter days, for us and for our salvation, born of the Virgin Mary ... according to the Manhood; one and the same Christ, Son, Lord, Only begotten, to be acknowledged in two natures, inconfusedly, unchangeably, indivisibly, inseparably ... as the prophets from the beginning have declared concerning him, and the Lord Jesus Christ himself has taught us, and the Creed of the holy Fathers has handed down to us".[7]

This "Chalcedonian Christology" has been ridiculed and dismissed as theological gobbledygook and logical nonsense by some. They think it absurd to affirm both the humanity and the deity of one person, a contradiction in terms. Yet this formulation is founded on and agreeable to the evidence concerning Jesus Christ presented in Holy Scripture. It is faithful to the facts narrated in the written word. Surely "the great, unthinkable, unimaginable miracle of the Incarnation which the Apostles proclaim is ... that the Eternal Son of God, who from all eternity was in the bosom of the Father, uncreated, Himself

---

6. Westminster Shorter Catechism, in *The Creeds of Christendom*, Q. 21 (III:680).

7. The Symbol of Chalcedon (451) in *The Creeds of Christendom*, II:62, 63.

proceeding from the Being of God Himself became man" and in His existence "manifests to us the Being of His Father".[8]

Beyond all doubt, the Bible affirms His true humanity. He was born into the world, cradled at Bethlehem, raised in Nazareth, heard in Galilee, seen in Judea, and crucified outside Jerusalem. He experienced hunger in the wilderness, thirst at Jacob's well in Samaria, anguish in the Garden of Gethsemane, and death at Calvary. It is also undoubtedly true that the Bible bears witness to His deity. He is eternal, divine, active in the work of creation, authorized and empowered to do what only God can do—forgive sins, raise the dead, and judge the world. He is "Immanuel, God with us" (Isa. 7:14). He is "God . . . manifested in the flesh" (I Tim. 3:16, KJV).

More than four centuries before Chalcedon, the apostle John declared: "In the beginning was the Word, and the Word was with God, and the Word was God. He was with God in the beginning. Through him were all things made; without him nothing was made that has been made . . . The Word became flesh and lived for a while among us. We have seen his glory, the glory of the one and only Son, who came from the Father, full of grace and truth" (John 1:1-3, 14). And the apostle Paul proclaimed Jesus Christ to be "in very nature God," and knew Him to possess "equality with God." He also understood that God's equal "made himself nothing, taking the very nature of a servant, being made in human likeness," that He might fulfil His saving mission on our behalf (Phil. 2:6-8). Is it any wonder that the apostle Thomas acknowledged and adored Him as "My Lord and my God"? (John 20:28).

Let us consider afresh the wonder of the incarnation and the person of Him who is indispensable to our salvation. Behold Him who was conceived by the Holy Ghost and born of the Virgin Mary. "There He is, for whom a heaven, suddenly swarming with all the notes of the antiphonal, offers the angels' impromptu chorus of 'Gloria in excelsis.' It is He who

---

8. Emil Brunner, *Dogmatics*, trans. Olive Wyon, 2 vols. (Philadelphia: The Westminster Press, 1950), II:356.

made the sun recoil and who tore from the mouth of the greatest of the prophets the names of Wonderful, Counselor, the Mighty God, the Everlasting Father, the Prince of Peace. It is only now, only today, that we can cry in truth, You are God among men!"[9]

PURPOSE

Why did the Son of God also become man? The incarnation was necessary that we might have a Mediator to reveal the invisible God to ignorant men and reconcile sinful men with a holy God.

One great purpose of His coming is related to revelation. The unseen God has given us clues as to His existence, power, goodness, wisdom, and holiness in the world of creation, the course of providence, and the voice of conscience. He has also sent us a series of spokesmen to bring us a word of judgment and hope. But through the incarnation He has done far more. "In the past, God spoke to our forefathers through the prophets at many times and in various ways, but in these last days he has spoken to us by his Son, whom he appointed heir of all things, and through whom he made the universe. The Son is the radiance of God's glory and the exact representation of his being" . . . (Heb. 1:1-3). He is "the image of God" and we can see "the light of the knowledge of the glory of God in the face of Christ" (II Cor. 4:4, 6). To behold the incarnate Son is to behold the invisible Father (John 14:9; 1:18).

The Son of God became man not only to reveal but also to reconcile. He came into the world to save sinners by removing the condemning factor of sin. This He did by direct involvement, personal commitment, and sacrificial identification. He absorbed into Himself the sins of His people and the judgment of God deserved by their sins, and so wrought reconciliation. Only the God-man could accomplish this. In the words of the

---

9. Paul Claudel, *I Believe in God* (New York: Holt, Rinehart & Winston, 1961) p. 51.

Larger Catechism drawn up by the Westminster Assembly in the 17th century, expressing the teaching of Holy Scripture, "It was requisite that the Mediator should be God, that he might sustain and keep the human nature from sinking under the infinite wrath of God, and the power of death; give worth and efficacy to his sufferings, obedience, and intercession; and to satisfy God's justice, procure his favour, purchase a peculiar people, give his Spirit to them, conquer all their enemies, and bring them to everlasting salvation".[10] And it was necessary that the Mediator should also be man, "that he might advance our nature, perform obedience to the law, suffer and make intercession for us in our nature, have a fellow-feeling of our infirmities; that we might receive the adoption of sons, and have comfort and access with boldness unto the throne of grace".[11]

We are not dependent on a mere man for our salvation, but rely on the unique God-man provided from heaven to be our Saviour. Jesus Christ "is not a saint offered up by humanity to God; He is the Son who has come from the Father into the world" to save sinners.[12] He is most certainly worthy of our trust, deserving of our love, and entitled to our obedience. He has come to be with us in the tasks, troubles, and temptations we face. We are not alone, for Jesus Christ is Emmanuel, God with us. He comes to dispel ignorance and overcome estrangement. He brings the light of revelation and the warmth of reconciliation. "Thanks be to God for his indescribable gift!" (II Cor. 9:15).

In Jesus Christ, the God-man, we have the Mediator we need. "It is Christ alone who joins heaven to earth. He alone is Mediator, reaching from heaven to the earth. He it is through whom the fullness of all heavenly gifts flows down to us and through whom we on our part may ascend to God... We who

10. Westminster Larger Catechism, Q. 38, *op. cit.*, III:684.

11. Ibid, Q. 39, III:684.

12. James Denney, *Studies in Theology* (London: Hodder & Stoughton, 1898) p. 51.

are firmly fixed not only upon the earth but in the abyss of the curse, and are submerged in hell itself, through him climb up to God"[13]

The Christ who came at Christmas will come again. This, too, is part of the Advent message. The worldly may mock and scoff, but we will affirm the promise of His coming as a certainty of faith. Let none "call in question what stands so plainly in the pages of the New Testament—what filled so exclusively the minds of the first Christians—the idea of a personal return of Christ at the end of the world ... if we are to retain any relation to the New Testament at all, we must assert the personal return of Christ as Judge of all"[14] Beyond affirmation of the doctrine, however, there must be preparation for the event. We prepare well for that encounter by repenting of our sins, and renewing our devotion to the doing of His will.

The Christ who came, and will come again, comes to us now. As His Word is preached and His Spirit moves upon our hearts, we know that He is with us in the time of worship. He goes with us as we obey the royal commission to make disciples of all nations for Him. He is our Lord Emmanuel, God ever with us.

HERALDING HIS INCARNATION

Prophets and apostles heralded the incarnation of the Son of God. Their message is epitomized in the word of the Lord's angel first addressed to Judean shepherds: "Do not be afraid. I bring you good news of great joy that will be for all the people. Today in the town of David a Saviour has been born to you; he is Christ the Lord. This will be a sign to you: You will find a baby wrapped in strips of cloth and lying in a manger" (Luke 2:10-12).

---

13. John Calvin, *Commentaries on the First Book of Moses called Genesis*, trans. John King, 2 vols. (Edinburgh: Calvin Translation Society, 1847) II:113 (on Gen. 28:12).

14. Denney, *Studies*, p. 329.

The Advent season, which begins four Sundays before Christmas, has a primary emphasis on the Christ who came in the fullness of time to save His people from their sins. It also includes reference to His return at the end to be our Judge, as well as the truth that He comes to us now by His Word and Spirit. Major attention, however, should be given to the wonder of the incarnation.

The Old Testament abounds in preaching material for the Advent season. Some of these texts have been grouped together in the opening section of Handel's oratorio, "Messiah." First performed in 1742 at Dublin, it has admirably survived both insensitive critics and some incompetent choirs. Here is "gospel music" at its very best, a marvelous marriage of the biblical message and appropriate music. What better way to prepare for the presentation of the Advent theme than to listen again to the Christmas portion of the oratorio, and then proceed to the exposition of passages drawn from it?

Handel's "Messiah" opens with the words of the fortieth chapter of Isaiah's prophecy, expressive of messianic hope. Over a period of weeks, you might present a sermon series based on Isaiah 40:1-11 along these lines:

40:1-2, where we have a message from the Lord, who is the ultimate Author of biblical revelation ("saith your God"); He is no dumb idol, but the living God who speaks; He makes himself known not only in the world of nature but particularly in the word of Scripture; God entrusts a message to His servants the prophets ("comfort ye"); the message of comfort is meant to put new heart into the covenant community ("my people"), after the disciplinary chastisement of the exile, with the assurance of the forgiveness of sins.

40:3-5, in which we hear the announcement of His advent; God is on the move, coming to Bethlehem in the person of Christ; descending at Pentecost in the presence of the Spirit; returning at the end to judge mankind through Christ; approaching us now, demanding a response of reception or rejection; note the preparation for His advent, by the plain preaching of the law of God (leveling human pride) and the compassionate offer of the gospel (lifting up the penitent); see also the result of His advent: the revelation of the glory of the Lord (see Ps. 19:1; Exod. 34:6, 7; John 1:14; II Cor. 4:6; Mark 8:38).

40:6-8, where we hear the note of realism ("all flesh is as grass"); change, decline, and decay are characteristic of civilizations, congregations, and individuals; even "the flower" fades — human excellence of beauty, strength, wealth, achievement are all subject to transiency; this should humble us; but then there's the note of optimism, rather than pessimism: "the word of our God endures for ever;" what He has promised, He will perform — whether it involves the liberation of Israel from the might of enslaving Babylon, or the redemption of His elect from the bondage of sin, death, and Satan; this "word" is none other than the gospel message of forgiveness and new life centered in Jesus Christ (I Peter 1:22-25).

40:9-11, in which we have a reference to the evangel ("good tidings") of release from the captivity of Babylon, reminding us of God's offer of freedom from the penalty and power of sin through the Christ who comes as a sovereign (judging righteously) and as a shepherd (tenderly caring for His flock); a reference, moreover, to the evangelists: the message is entrusted to "Zion" or "Jerusalem," to be shared with "the cities of Judah"; all God's people should be involved in the spread of the gospel, not just a few gifted evangelists (Eph. 4:11; Acts 1:8); every Christian should communicate the Christian message by word and deed, with clarity, conviction, and compassion to "the cities" of our time.

The reverent and relevant exposition of these biblical texts will prove as rewarding to the preacher in the course of preparation as for the congregation in the moment of delivery. Other Old Testament promises regarding the Messiah, so appropriate for the heralding of the incarnation, include:

Isaiah 7:14, the prophecy of the miraculous conception by the mysterious work of the Spirit and the Saviour's birth of the Virgin; also the indication of the Child's uniqueness as "Emmanuel," God-with-us, sharing our griefs, touched with our infirmities, encountering our temptations, bearing our sins (Matt. 1:18-25).

Isaiah 9:6, 7 - here the "name" of the Child born to Mary, and the Son given by God, is presented as "Wonderful Counselor" (by

His Word and Spirit of truth, in contrast to false religions and deceitful counselors); "the Mighty God" (hero of our redemption, deserving of adoration); "the Everlasting Father" (fatherly tenderness and benevolence in dealing with our weakness); "the Prince of Peace" (restoring the broken relationship with God, the disrupted fellowship with others, the inner serenity of the soul disturbed by guilt and fear).

Malachi 3:1-3, in which there is a prediction of the preparatory ministry of John the Baptist (the messenger sent to clear the way for Him who is the Way); and a declaration of Christ's mission in terms of purification designed to make our service to God possible and acceptable.

Malachi 4:2, where the Messiah is described as "the Sun of Righteousness" whose rising on the landscape of history brings light to those in darkness, and healing to those affected by the dread disease of sin.

Isaiah 35:1-6, foretelling Messiah's merciful ministry to men in need; fulfilled in the course of gospel history through actual miracles (Matthew 11:2-5) which also serve as credentials in support of the claims of Jesus to be the Christ, and as illustrations of the way in which gospel grace operates on human personality to restore the wholeness ruined by sin.

Micah 5:1-4, where the Messiah is described as both shepherd (caring for His people) and sovereign (ruling with authority over all); significantly, the birthplace of Him who is the Bread of God, the Bread of Heaven, the Bread of Life, is to be Bethlehem: "the house of bread."

Beginning with the "protevangelium" in Genesis 3:15, we need to search and study the Scriptures so that we may present Jesus Christ in a new way from the Old Testament.

When we turn to the New Testament, we find a wealth of sermonic material for use in several successive Advent seasons. Consider, for example, the treasure trove preserved by Luke in the first two chapters of His gospel:

1:1-4, a prologue consisting of but a single sentence in the original Greek text, confronting us with several basic considerations of the utmost importance; first, that Christian faith is founded on redemptive history (rather than on feelings or fables, it rests on facts, events with credible witnesses); second, that redemptive history is recorded in Holy Scripture (the narration of a physician-historian whose accuracy has been abundantly confirmed); third, that Holy Scripture is given for personal assurance (whether of Theophilus in apostolic times, or ourselves today).

1:46-56, "Magnificat," a carol of Christmas so named because of its opening word in the Latin version; listen to Mary as theologian, praising the God of experience (her Lord, her Saviour); the God of history (who has abased the proud and exalted the humble); the God of prophecy (who has promised help to His people and now kept that promise in sending the Saviour).

1:67-80, another carol of Christmas, "Benedictus," sung by a Spirit-filled priest named Zacharias; it declares several great truths about God: He speaks (living, articulate, able to perform what He has promised); He saves (active for the good of His people, visiting and redeeming them); He sends (both the servant: John the Baptist, and the Son: Jesus Christ).

2:14, "Gloria in excelsis," carol of the angelic choir on the night of the Saviour's birth; "peace" is now a reality for men on earth because of the Saviour's coming; God's "good-will" has provided Jesus, a Gift undeserved by us; let there be "glory" to God, praise and thanksgiving, with sacred joy, for His inexpressible Gift.

2:29-35, "Nunc dimittis," the fourth carol preserved by Luke, expresses the contentment of an aged saint who holds the infant Christ in his arms; Jesus has come for all men, Jews and Gentiles; some will receive Him and be saved, others will reject Him and be lost; this rejection, culminating in the cross, will bring sorrow to the soul of Mary.

Reference has already been made to the historical narrative in Matthew 1:18-25, recording the fulfillment of what the prophet had said in Isaiah 7:14. Also in Matthew's account is the story of the Magi who sought the new-born King, and the wicked ruler who resorted to violence because he feared Jesus as a rival (2:1-12). This text is appropriate for Epiphany (the thirteenth day after Christmas, the 6th of January) or the Sunday nearest to it. The episode contains an important message that declares the world-wide nature of the Christian gospel. God's saving grace makes its epiphany or appearance in Christ, offering hope to all people everywhere (Titus 2:11).

Rather than become sentimental over stars, camels, or "the three kings," concentrate on the key point: the manifestation of the glory of God in Jesus Christ even to the Gentiles who come from afar (recall Isa. 40:3-5). This is an intensely missionary text. It is also a wonderful evangelistic text. Stress that wise men still seek Him, and that it is our responsibility to show them where He may surely be found.

Other advent messages may be drawn from the statements of Jesus regarding His own mission in the world, as these are recorded in the gospels. A concordance will show many passages which mention His being "sent" by the Father, or of having "come" for the fulfillment of a purpose.

In the Synoptics, for example, you will find references to the reason for His incarnation in texts such as Luke 4:18, 19, or Matthew 9:13, or Mark 10:45. Survey the references, select some for closer study, then expound upon them in an appropriate order during the weeks leading up to Christmas.

The gospel of John also abounds in Advent material, revealing the purpose of His coming in words as significant as they are familiar. Consider, for instance, John 3:15-17, 6:32-40, 9:1-7, and 10:1-18.

What has been suggested for the gospels can also be said regarding the epistles. They are filled with clear and compelling testimony concerning the purpose of His coming, and are indispensable to "keeping Christ in Christmas." Think of passages such as Galatians 4:4-7, I Timothy 1:15, Hebrews 2:14-18, I John 4:7-11, or that grand summary of Christ's person and work in I Timothy 3:16.

When heralding the incarnation, never lose sight of the following factors: expectation, event, explanation, ethics, and renewed expectation. Attention to these will keep us from missing the message and depriving God's people of the fullness of the gospel at the Advent season.

Expectation: God's promise of a Saviour, revealed through His servants the prophets.

Event: God's fulfillment of His promise in the actual coming of the Messiah, who was conceived of the Holy Spirit and born of the Virgin Mary, becoming man without ceasing to be God's equal.

Explanation: Gospel history has a saving significance, doctrine is the authentic interpretation of the event, and is also given by divine revelation through prophets and apostles; He came to save His people from their sins.

Ethics: What happened was meant to have a practical bearing on our personal character and social relationships. Beyond doctrine but because of doctrine, emphasize duty motivated by gratitude for grace revealed in Christ.

Expectation: The Christ who came will come again to complete the redemptive process with the defeat of death, the resurrection of the body, and the judgment of the world in righteousness.

Not all of these factors will be present in every text, but wherever they occur, we should not fail to deal with them adequately. We must, moreover, never forget that the biblical message is meant for real people — men and women who face tasks and temptations, encounter difficulties, endure disappointments, fall short of God's standard, and are overshadowed by mortality. We need to know that we are not alone, that God is with us in Jesus Christ, our Emmanuel.

While the Advent message must be derived from the careful exegesis of Scripture and presented through relevant exposition, it should prove helpful to read sermons prepared by other preachers on the text.

Canon H. P. Liddon of St. Paul's Cathedral in London was a scholarly and prolific writer whose sermons, delivered during the latter part of the nineteenth century, are still informative and interesting. In the volume entitled "Christmastide In St. Paul's," he dealt with many texts particularly appropriate to the Advent season.

Preaching on I Timothy 3:16, "God in Human Form," he noted that "the Apostle's words to Timothy put before us forcibly and concisely the master-truth which gives Christmas its

meaning".[15] The God who manifests Himself in nature, conscience, and providence actually entered time and space in the
person of Jesus Christ. He came to reveal the unseen God to
us, and reconcile us to the holy God. Expounding John 1:14,
"The Word Made Flesh," Liddon explained the meaning of "the
greatest birthday in the year"[16] as consisting in the fact that
the Eternal Son was born as Mary's child. Quoting from the
Nicene and Athanasian Creeds as well as the Te Deum, he
underlined the truth of the two natures in the one person of
Jesus Christ so essential for our salvation.

Liddon's sermon on Revelation 21:3, "The Incarnate God
With Men," develops the theme of the divine presence through
the pillar of cloud and fire, in the tabernacle, and the temple of
the Old Testament. It also points to Jesus Christ as the One in
whom the fullness of the Godhead dwells bodily, radiant with
grace and truth, and declares that the same God is present now
in the company of believers (Matt. 28:20; Col. 1:27), and will
dwell in "the glorified Church of His living members," at the
end.[17]

"Born of a Woman" is the title of Liddon's sermon on Galatians 4:4. The Son was sent forth from the very depths of deity,
and willingly put Himself within reach of His creatures. That
He was born of a woman, without mention of Joseph's role, is
interpreted as an indirect testimony to the truth of the miraculous conception and virgin birth of Jesus Christ. Preaching on
the theme, "Born of a Virgin," Matthew 1:22, 23, Liddon con-
cluded: "What is my actual relation to Him, who, for the love of
me was conceived of the Holy Ghost, and born of the Virgin
Mary; my present Redeemer and my future Judge?"[18]

In "The Guidance of the Star," based on Matthew 2:1, 2, Liddon sees the coming of the Magi to the cradle of Christ as a

---

15. H.P. Liddon, *Christmastide in St. Paul's* (London: Longmans, Green, 1890)
p. 107.

16. Ibid, p. 123.

17. Ibid, p. 153.

18. Ibid, p. 106.

fulfillment of prophecies such as Psalm 86:9; 22:27, 28; Isaiah 11:1, 10; 46:6; 60:3. He points out the variety of ways in which God leads people to Christ: through a star, the influence of a friend or relative, a verse of Scripture, a public event, the message of a book. He also recognizes the importance of acting on as much of the truth as we know, step by step, if we would come to an encounter with Christ. Above all, we must discern in Jesus Christ the suffering sovereign whose deity deserves worship. Liddon concludes, "Oh! send out Thy light and Thy truth, Eternal Jesus, and bring us at this blessed season unto Thy holy hill and to Thy dwelling; and we will go, in this our pilgrimage through time, to the Altar of God, even unto the God of our joy and gladness; and through Thy grace and mercy, in the eternity beyond, upon the harp will we give thanks unto Thee, O Lord our God"![19]

The music of the Advent season helps to herald the incarnation. Hymns that tell the message of Messiah's birth and the meaning of His coming should be featured. Those that do otherwise ought to be avoided. Appropriate selections from Handel's "Messiah" will enrich the worship experience. Not every church, however, may have an organist, choir, and soloists capable of doing this with competence as well as conviction.

Of the many hymns commemorating and celebrating the nature and purpose of the incarnation is this one written by Charles Wesley in 1743:

> Hark! the herald angels sing
> Glory to the new-born King,
> Peace on earth, and mercy mild,
> God and sinners reconciled.
> Joyful, all ye nations, rise;
> Join the triumph of the skies;
> With the angelic host proclaim,
> "Christ is born in Bethlehem."
>
> Christ, by highest heaven adored,
> Christ, the Everlasting Lord,

---

19. Ibid, p. 367.

> Late in time behold Him come,
> Offspring of a Virgin's womb.
> Veiled in flesh the Godhead see!
> Hail the Incarnate Deity!
> Pleased as Man with men to dwell,
> Jesus, our Emmanuel.
>
> Hail, the heaven-born Prince of Peace!
> Hail, the Sun of Righteousness!
> Light and life to all He brings,
> Risen with healing in His wings.
> Mild, He lays His glory by,
> Born that man no more may die,
> Born to raise the sons of earth,
> Born to give them second birth.
>
> Hark! the herald angels sing
> Glory to the new-born King.

This hymn is a good example of fidelity to Scripture stirringly expressed. The same may be said of hymns like "As with Gladness Men of Old," "Brightest and Best," "Hark, the Glad Sound," and the paraphrase of Isaiah 9:1-7, "The Race that Long in Darkness Pined." "It Came Upon a Midnight Clear," however enjoyable its tune, fails to make any clear reference to the Christ without whom there would be no Christmas. Why continue to use it when there are so many other biblical carols for the Advent season?

One hymn which is applicable to both the first and second advents of our Lord is, "O Come, O Come, Emmanuel." For many centuries, it has expressed the Christian hope centered in Jesus the Redeemer. The same is true of Wesley's "Come, Thou Long-expected Jesus."

Praise selections such as "Christians, Awake! Salute the Happy Morn," "Joy to the World," "O Little Town of Bethlehem," and "O Come, All Ye Faithful," along with "Silent Night," are perennial favorites. It is regrettable that their use is generally limited to a few occasions concentrated in the closing weeks of each December. What God did in sending His beloved Son, and what Christ accomplished by coming into the world, is a wonder worthy of joyful praise all the days of our years.

LENT

2

Christ For Us

Proclaiming His Redemption

Jesus Christ is Emmanuel, God come down to earth, sharing our frailty and mortality to liberate us from the penalty and power of our iniquity. He was born into the world to save His people from their sins. Incarnation was, therefore, not only revelation but also redemption. He came to reveal the unseen God and redeem sinful men. He came not alone to reveal but also to reconcile. In the words of the Nicene Creed, formulated in the fourth century, we believe in the Lord Jesus Christ, "the only-begotten Son of God, begotten of the Father before all worlds, God of God, Light of Light, very God of very God, begotten, not made, being of one essence with the Father; by whom all things were made; who, for us men and for our salvation, came down from heaven, and was incarnate by the Holy Ghost of the Virgin Mary, and was made man".[1]

---

1. The Nicene Creed (381) in *The Creeds of Christendom*, compiled Philip Schaff, 3 vols. (New York: Harper & Brothers , 1877) II:58, 59.

But how did Christ, the Word thus made flesh, accomplish His saving mission? The Redeemer of God's elect accomplished the work of salvation by fulfilling His messianic ministry as our prophet, priest, and king.

By His prophetic service, Jesus reveals to us the will of God for our salvation. His Spirit, speaking to us in the Scriptures, teaches us with infallible authority about the duty, depravity, dignity, and destiny of man. He summons us to faith and repentance so that we do not perish in our sins but receive forgiveness and new life.

In His royal office or function, Christ the King of Glory subdues us to Himself. He rules and defends us. He restrains and conquers all His enemies and ours, including death and the devil. All power belongs to Him in heaven and on earth. He is the Head of the new community, the Church, and shall be revealed as supreme Lord at His coming. Then shall our blessed hope be fulfilled. Then shall we know the fullness of the righteousness, holiness, and happiness of His Kingdom.

It is particularly in His priestly ministry, however, that Christ makes Himself known as our Saviour. He did all that needed doing to save us from the penalty and power of sin by His unique sacrifice of Himself on the altar of the cross, and now continues the work of mercy as He intercedes for us in heaven.

The Westminster Confession of Faith sums up His saving mission in these words: "The Lord Jesus, by his perfect obedience and sacrifice of himself, which he through the eternal Spirit once offered up to God, hath fully satisfied the justice of his Father; and purchased not only reconciliation, but an everlasting inheritance in the kingdom of heaven, for all those whom the Father hath given unto him."[2]

This involves an experience of reconciliation and the reception of an everlasting inheritance by all who believe the gospel. But this experience is only possible because of something that

---

2. Westminster Confession of Faith (1647) in *The Creeds of Christendom*, ch. 8:5 (III:621).

has actually happened in the course of history—a historical reality with a definite doctrinal significance. It is not simply that Christ was born and that He died, but that He died to deliver us from the condemnation and corruption of sin—this is the firm basis of our hope for time and eternity.

Let us always remember that Christianity is "not just a way of life . . . but a way of life founded upon a message. It was based, not upon mere feeling, not upon a mere program of work, but upon an account of facts . . . It was based upon doctrine."[3] Without these two elements of history and doctrine indissolubly joined, there is no biblical Christianity.

Undoubtedly, "the work of Christ in relation to sin is the great thing in the gospel."[4] Indeed, "at the heart of Christianity there is a cross, and on that cross the Son of God wrought man's salvation."[5] Let us take a fresh look at the historical reality of His death as narrated in the Scriptures, and consider again the doctrinal meaning of that death. To recall the event is not enough. It is the event's significance that makes the fact of Calvary a gospel for sinners in need of grace.

We focus, then, on the death of Christ. According to the Scriptures, it is a sacrifice whose character is voluntary, vicarious, and valuable.

VOLUNTARY

In thinking of the passion and death of our Lord, we become aware of man's indifference and hostility to Him. We hear crafty Caiaphas conspiring against the Son of God, and we listen as Judas negotiates the price of betrayal. We see Pontius Pilate, unscrupulous politician dedicated to his own ends,

---

3. J. Gresham Machen, *Christianity and Liberalism*, 1923. (Grand Rapids: Eerdmans, n.d.) p. 21.

4. James Denney, *Studies in Theology* (London: Hodder & Stoughton, 1898) p. 125.

5. Leon Morris, "The Atonement" in *Basic Christian Doctrines*, ed. C.F.H. Henry (New York: Holt, Rinehart & Winston, 1962) p. 152.

and that sensual sovereign distinguished by superstition, Herod of Galilee. We recall the opposition of scribes, elders, Pharisees, Sadducees, soldiers, slaves, priests, and masses manipulated by apostate demagogues.

Yet in the final analysis Jesus is not the unfortunate victim of brute force or malicious men. He endures the anguish of betrayal, mockery, false accusation, flagellation, rejection, crucifixion, derision, and death willingly. His passion and death are voluntary. He did this in love so as to accomplish His saving work. It was all "for us men, and for our salvation."

It was not coercion or compulsion from without but compassion from within that led Him from heaven to earth and from Galilee to Calvary. When we see Jesus "conflicting with the indignities of the world, the temptations of Satan, and the infirmities in his flesh . . . betrayed by Judas, forsaken by his disciples, scorned and rejected by the world, condemned by Pilate, and tormented by his persecutors . . . enduring the terrors of death and the powers of darkness" let us remember that He willingly laid down his life as an offering for sin on His cross.[6]

Surely the gospel tells of the Father's love in giving the Son to be our Saviour (Rom. 8:32; 5:8; John 3:16). But it also dwells on the fact that the Son of God loved us and gave Himself for us, willingly enduring the painful, shameful, and accursed death of the cross (Gal. 2:20; 3:13). Such love compels us to love Him in return, and serve Him with faithfulness no matter what the cost (II Cor. 5:14; I John 4:19).

The death of Jesus Christ at Calvary was voluntary. His crucifixion climaxed His incarnation. He did it willingly because He was concerned with the plight of sinners under the judgment of a holy and righteous God (John 10:18; Phil. 2:5-8).

---

6. Westminster Larger Catechism, in *A Harmony of the Westminster Presbyterian Standards*, compiled J.B. Green (Richmond: John Knox Press, 1965) Q. 48, 49 (pp. 58, 59).

VICARIOUS

The passion and death of our Lord were not only voluntary, but vicarious. What Jesus did, He did *for* others. As we consider what the Spirit says about this in the Scriptures, we become aware of the fact that *for* is the most significant preposition of the gospel.

The Gospel presupposes the bad news of man's sin and God's judgment. Because we have sinned, we deserve to be expelled from the presence of God and exposed to the revelation of His wrath. But we can be acquitted of all the charges hanging over us and be accepted into the fellowship of God's family, through faith in this Saviour.

The person of Christ cannot be separated from the work of Christ. Had Jesus been a sinner, He could not have wrought righteousness in His life nor made atonement in His death. He would have been in the very same predicament as ourselves.[7]

It is of the utmost importance that we have a clear understanding of the evangelical significance of that historical event which took place outside the city walls of Jerusalem more than nineteen centuries ago. And that evangelical significance centers in the word *for*, the great preposition of the passion.

Consider the scriptural evidence for the gospel message that Christ died to save us from the condemnation and corruption of sin. Recall first the Old Testament teaching on the holiness of God, the sinfulness of man, and the reality of God's wrath against sinners. Think also of the reality of God's grace. The Lord provided a way out. Over the head of a sacrificial lamb, sins would be confessed and guilt symbolically transferred. Then the lamb would be slain and the sinner spared, signifying that iniquity had been punished through the death of a substitute (Lev. 16:11). The prophet Isaiah spoke of the suffering servant who would be "wounded for our transgressions, and

---

7. Gordon H. Clark, *What Presbyterians Believe* (Philadelphia: Presbyterian & Reformed, 1965) p. 97.

bruised for our iniquities." Christ, our sacrifice and substitute, would take onto himself the burden of our guilt and the weight of God's judgment (Isa. 53:4-7).

The New Testament gives explicit expression to the doctrine of vicarious atonement. Only a virtuoso in exegetical evasion could fail to find this gospel truth plainly presented in its pages.

John the Baptist introduces Jesus as the Lamb of God who has come on the scene of history to deal with the problem of the world's sin (John 1:29, 35). Peter proclaims that Jesus is the spotless lamb offered up in sacrifice to liberate us from the judgment of God and the bondage of sin (I Peter 1:18-20). He sees Jesus as the innocent sufferer wounded for others, just as Isaiah had prophesied (I Peter 2:24). He declares that the righteous Jesus has suffered for the unjust, in order to remove the barrier of sin and open the way to reconciliation with a holy God (I Peter 3:18).

The apostle John tells us of the forgiveness and cleansing of the blood of Jesus Christ, the Son of God. He declares that the death of Christ should be understood as a sacrifice, an act of propitiation meant to turn away the divine displeasure and restore us to fellowship with the Father (I John 1:7-2:2).

Paul constantly refers to the vicarious sacrifice of Christ on the cross. He not only narrates history, saying that "Christ died," but immediately adds the authentic explanation of that event: "for our sins" (I Cor. 15:3). Christ has redeemed us from the curse of the law we sinners had broken, "by becoming a curse for us" (Gal. 3:13). "God ... reconciled us to himself through Christ—not counting men's sins against them ... God made him who had no sin to be sin for us, so that in him we might become the righteousness of God" (II Cor. 5:18, 19, 21). Although all have sinned and fallen short of the glory of God, yet everyone who believes in Christ shall be spared from judgment and restored to fellowship. Why? Because of what Christ has done for sinners in His atoning death. We are saved through faith in Him who made the sacrifice for us (Rom. 3:21-26).

The author of the letter to the Hebrews declares that the death of Christ must be understood in terms of vicarious sacrifice and substitution. Not only does this correspondence make repeated reference to the Old Testament background of priest and sacrifice, but it clearly affirms that Christ is both priest and sacrifice. In His unique death on the altar of the cross, He made atonement for the sins of His people (Heb. 7:26, 27; 9:11-14; 10:11, 12).

What is taught by prophets and apostles is surely true to the teaching of Jesus. He interprets His death as a sacrifice, both voluntary and vicarious. The Good Shepherd gives His life for the sheep. He lays down His life with sovereign freedom and limitless love (John 10:11, 17). He institutes a memorial of His death, saying that the bread represents that body broken for us, and the cup reminds us of blood shed to atone for sins so that the covenant relationship with God is restored (Matt. 26:26-28). Jesus says that "the Son of Man did not come to be served, but to serve, and to give his life a ransom for many" (Mark 10:45).

Despite the overwhelming evidence in the Scriptures supporting the gospel understanding of the death of Christ as a vicarious sacrifice, there are some professors and preachers who distort and discard this doctrine as unworthy of their concept of God. One theologian, for instance, considers it unbiblical to say that Christ satisfied the justice of God for sinners. Ascribing that teaching to Anselm (1033-1109) as its inventor, he charges: "The theology of Anselm ... that the sacrifice of Christ fulfilled a legal requirement on the part of God, is incompatible with the central evangelical message of the New Testament, that forgiveness is the free gift of God, that it flows spontaneously from his love, and that it does not first have to be procured from him by the fulfillment of some condition on the part of Christ".[8]

---

8. G. S. Hendry, *The Westminster Confession for Today* (London: SCM Press, 1960) p. 112.

Another author refers to the propitiation, ransom, and penal interpretations of the death of Christ, and then concludes: "We can reject these various theories of a blood atonement for their artificiality, for sin is certainly not like a money transaction which can be paid by someone else. They suggest a vengeful, arbitrary God".[9]

One can only hold such views as authentic biblical teaching by disregarding or denying what the Word of God actually says. These views ignore the truth of the holiness of God and the necessity of sacrifice — vicarious sacrifice — for the salvation of sinners declared in Scripture. "Without the shedding of blood there is no forgiveness . . . Christ was sacrificed once to take away the sins of many people" (Heb. 9:22, 28).

A god who condones sin is not the holy and just God of the Bible but an idol created by human sentiment or speculation. It would be totally inconsistent with the purity and righteousness of the true and living God for Him to permit sin to pass with impunity. The punishment of sin in the person of Christ, far from being the invention of Anselm, is a moral necessity according to the Scriptures. Our Saviour suffered all that was necessary to demonstrate God's hatred of sin, to vindicate the authority of God's law, and to exclude the impenitent from the hope of grace.

The truth of the atonement, moreover, does not involve an arbitrary or vengeful deity, but a gracious and merciful Father who gives His beloved Son to make atonement, and a Son who yields Himself for us in sacrifical love.

We must affirm this truth today, else we will have no good news for sinful man. "From the earliest ages Christians have believed that Christ's death was an atonement for sin, a sacrifice offered to God to satisfy his justice, and avert his wrath from the guilty; that it was the means of reconciling us to our offended Creator, the procuring cause of pardon and life".[10]

---

9.   Georgia Harkness, *Understanding the Christian Faith* (Nashville: Abingdon-Cokesbury, 1947) p. 31.

10. John Dick, *Lectures on Theology*, 2 vols. (New York: Robert Carter & Brothers, 1851) II:57.

VICTORIOUS

The death of Christ was not only voluntary and vicarious, but victorious. The Victim was also Victor. This triumphant aspect of our Lord's death is presented by Paul when he says that God "forgave us all our sins, having canceled the written code, with all its regulations, that was against us and that stood opposed to us; he took it away, nailing it to the cross. And having disarmed the powers and authorities, he made a public spectacle of them, triumphing over them by the cross" (Col. 2:13-15). In the death of the cross, Christ accomplished God's redemptive purpose faithfully and victoriously.

This is the triumph of Christ, wrought in the depths of the valley of the shadow of death. "The humiliation of Christ manifests the greatness of his love, the riches of his grace. It was for us men, and for our salvation, that he assumed human nature, and abased himself to the dust of death. He drew a veil over his glory that he might remove our reproach, and raise us to heavenly honours; he groaned and died, that we might obtain immortal felicity".[11]

Something actually happened on that cross to change our situation as sinners condemned of God. At Calvary, there occurred "an objective transaction which changed the human situation".[12] Now, through faith in Christ, we are justified — acquitted and accepted of God.

In the Old Testament story, when the blood of the slain lamb was applied to the door post of an Israelite home, that family was spared by the angel of judgment. The messenger of God's wrath passed over those who were thus protected by the blood of sacrifice. In the New Testament, we have the blessed assurance that those to whom the benefits of Christ's sacrifice have been applied shall be spared from doom. There is no condemnation awaiting believers who rely on Christ for salvation (Rom.

---

11. Ibid, II:100.

12. James S. Stewart, *A Faith to Proclaim* (London: Hodder & Stoughton, 1952) p. 84.

8:1). They experience redemption, release from guilt, the freedom of forgiveness, through faith in Him whose blood was shed for them at Calvary (Eph. 1:7).

Forgiveness is necessary because we have sinned against God. Guilt troubles us. Broken commitments and shattered relationships weigh heavily upon the conscience. We sense our alienation from God and from one another, and we cannot stand the scrutiny of His searching eyes. But forgiveness is possible, because Christ has exposed Himself to the judgment deserved by our sins, and died in our place. Now, through faith in Him as our substitute and sacrifice, we are acquitted. The charges against us are dropped. The indictment is quashed.

Our acquittal, then, is dependent on the saving work of Christ, who "took upon Himself the dreadful guilt of our sins and bore it instead of us on the cross".[13]

But the gospel offers us more than acquittal. A criminal can have his case dismissed and still be treated as an outcast by society. Not so in the eyes of the pardoning God. All who trust in Christ as Saviour are not only forgiven but welcomed into the fellowship of His family. They are regarded as sons, and are given an everlasting inheritance. This acceptance, this reconciliation, this peace with God, is all experienced through faith in Christ crucified (Rom. 5:1). His death is the propitiation for our sins, averting the wrath of God and securing instead the Father's favor.

Christ, as our sin-bearer, was willing to be forsaken that we might be restored to fellowship with God. He died to open the gate for us into the family of God. He is the bridge over the troubled waters that fill the abyss between the sin of man and the holiness of God. He is our mediator, and our peace, through the blood of His cross (I Tim. 2:5, 6; Col. 1:20).

We see, then, that "a new face has been put on life by the blessed thing that God did when He offered up His only begotten Son".[14] This is the theme of true gospel preaching, and the

---

13. Machen, *op. cit.*, p. 117.
14. Ibid, p. 70.

message of real gospel music. The preaching that moves heart, mind, and will is not a matter of cleverness, eloquence, or wit. Evangelistic preaching is the announcement of what God has graciously done for us in Christ, calling on sinners to repent and to believe the gospel centering in His cross (I Cor. 2:1-5).

PREACHING HIS REDEMPTION

In what are known as "liturgical churches," the Lenten season begins with Ash Wednesday, forty days before Easter (excluding Sundays). Traditionally observed as a period of self-denial and meditation on our Lord's passion and death, Lent can deepen the devotion of disciples who concentrate on Jesus Christ and His crucifixion.

The evangelical (rather than merely ritual) observance of Lent brings great spiritual benefits because it majors in the very centralities of the evangel: God's holiness and love, revealed at Calvary, through the Christ who bore in His own body our sins on the cross and accomplished the work of redemption.

In the Old Testament, there are many passages prophetic of His passion. Our Lord encourages us so to interpret "Moses and all the prophets" (Luke 24:27). Think, for example, of the prophecies given in Isaiah 53, portraying not only the sufferings of the Lord's Servant, but indicating the saving significance of His death:

53:1-3, the sorrow of Christ; God's message is rejected by those who doubt or deny its truth, and thus fail to experience its saving power; God's Messiah is also rejected by a world unappreciative of His worth and oblivious to its desperate need of Him.

53:4-6, the sacrifice of Christ; see the misunderstanding of the cross by those who considered the Sufferer as a blasphemous impostor who deserved to die; note also the meaning of the cross, in terms of vicarious sacrifice for the sins of others.

53:7-8, the silence of Christ; oppressed, yet He responds with neither complaint, nor curse, nor compromise, but submission

(I Peter 2:18-25); His passive silence, however, is also powerful: how dreadful is the plight of Herod, Pilate, the priests, and the Sanhedrin to whom Christ has nothing more to say!

53:9-12, the sovereignty of Christ; review His obedience, so voluntary, vicarious, and victorious; consider the reward of His obedience: after the cross, the crown; after humiliation, exaltation; after condemnation, vindication for Himself and justification for His people.

The prophecy of Zechariah is rich in predictions of our Saviour's redemptive sufferings, yet rarely are any of them expounded by the contemporary pastor. Though we profess to believe in the plenary as well as verbal inspiration of Scripture, Zechariah and the other "minor" prophets are often neglected. But here is testimony to Christ deserving of disciplined study and devotional exposition:

9:9-10, the prophecy about the King of righteousness and peace, fulfilled on the first Palm Sunday.

11:12-13, the low esteem in which the Shepherd of Israel was held, paid thirty pieces of silver for His services, pointing ahead to the treachery of Judas who sold the Master for precisely that sum.

12:10, a moving reference to the work of the Spirit who leads us to heartbroken repentance through a contemplation of Him through whom our sins have pierced, beginning at Pentecost (Acts 2:37).

13:1, where we have the announcement that a fountain for the cleansing of personality pollution due to sin is now opened; in the light of I John 1:7, 9 we rightly see this as a promise of cleansing grace fulfilled through Christ crucified as His saving sacrifice is applied to the need of penitent believers.

Study the Psalms in preparation for preaching during the season leading up to Good Friday. The twenty-second Psalm, quoted by our Saviour as He suffered on the cross, is an amazing prophecy of His passion and triumph. Remembering that the true Lenten fast acceptable to God does not consist in mere abstinence from meat but the crucifixion of "the flesh" and all its unruly desires (Gal. 5:24), let us expound the penitential

Psalms. These focus on man's sin, God's displeasure, and the gospel's promise of pardon with the joy of restored relationships. In this connection, think of Psalms such as 32, 38, 39, 51, and 130.

Before turning to the New Testament revelation and its message of redemption wrought by Jesus Christ, some reference should be made to the writings of Moses. The Pentateuch also proclaims Messiah's passion. Recall the story of the Passover, the liberation from slavery through the Exodus, the priesthood and sacrifices of the tabernacle — all these point forward to Christ our Redeemer. They never fail to enrich God's people when relevantly expounded.

In the New Testament revelation, we see Jesus Christ most clearly presented. The Father points us to His beloved Son, and the Spirit draws us to the Saviour's side. Our preaching ought to be Christocentric, with due regard for the trinitarian framework of biblical revelation.

In successive Lenten seasons, present the passion and death of our Lord through the eyes of each of the evangelists. During the first year, begin with Mark's account. Trace the movement to Calvary as recorded in that graphic gospel, rightly called a transcript from life. The next year, follow the way of the cross as told by Matthew. The third year, look at the journey to Jerusalem and the cross with Luke as your guide. In the fourth year, let John direct your thoughts to contemplate the Lamb of God, slain on that altar at Calvary to bear away the sin of the world.

Draw on material provided by each of the evangelists in successive Lenten seasons, using it over a period of weeks in every instance, or beginning with the entry into Jerusalem on Palm Sunday and continuing through each night of Holy Week to Good Friday. Whatever plan you follow, concentrate on preaching Christ. Present "Jesus Christ and him crucified" (I Cor. 2:2).

The gospel record abounds in sayings and events related to the climax of redemption at the cross. Some year, rather than systematically expounding the story as presented by Matthew, Mark, Luke, or John, you may plan to cut across the gospels and prepare a series on the seven words spoken by Christ from the pulpit of Calvary:

Luke 23:34, the plea of the merciful Christ who makes intercession for the transgressors.

Luke 23:39-43, the gift of the sovereign Lord who gave a penitent thief the promise of paradise.

John 19:25-27, the wish of the beloved Son who cared for His mother and committed her to the new community of faith.

Mark 15:33, 34, the lament of the desolate Sufferer who was forsaken that we might be restored to fellowship with God.

John 19:28, 29, the desire of the crucified Christ who experienced thirst that we might have the water of life everlasting.

John 19:30, the cry of the conqueror who has accomplished redemption, obedient unto death, even the death of the cross, to atone for the sins of His people.

Luke 23:46, the prayer of the confident Jesus who commended His spirit into the hands of the Father and thus robbed death of its terrors.

In *The Light of the Cross*, S. Barton Babbage presents a series of studies in the persons who appeared in the gospel story, particularly as they stand revealed with reference to Christ crucified:

The governor Pilate — skeptical unbelief
The priest Caiaphas — cynical opportunism
The tetrarch Herod — moral degeneration
The traitor Judas — bitter remorse
The penitent thief — saving faith
The beloved John — unholy ambition
The blessed Mary — humble submission
The scribe Mark — spiritual rehabilitation
The Roman centurion — unsolicited testimony
The robber Barabbas — unmerited pardon
The ruler Nicodemus — secret discipleship
Mary Magdalene — love's devotion

Peter the rock — love's impulsiveness
Joseph of Arimathea — sinful procrastination
Saul the Pharisee — sovereign grace![15]

Life Through the Cross by Marcus Loane, Archbishop of the Sydney Diocese of the Anglican Church in Australia, follows the course of events from our Lord's agony in Gethsemane's garden to His resurrection from the grave in Joseph's garden![16] In presenting the Man of Sorrows, he preaches sermons entitled The Olive Grove, The Broken Cry, The Father's Will, The Darkest Hour, The Heedless Three, The Stricken Band, The Traitor's Kiss, The Naked Sword, The Wanton Blow, The False Witness, The Solemn Oath, and The Last Verdict. The next group of sermons, under the heading of The Crown of Thorns, shows us Christ on trial, condemned to die. Throughout, this faithful preacher of our Lord's passion points us to the Redeemer's "full, perfect, and sufficient sacrifice, oblation, and satisfaction for the sins of the whole world." The gospel message comes through clearly: the Son of God loved us, and gave Himself for us sinners, dying the death we deserved to die.

Friedrich Wilhelm Krummacher was not only a professor of theology and speech but a distinguished preacher of the Word in the Germany of the early nineteenth century. A defender of the gospel in a time of rising rationalism and unbelief, he proclaimed the message of the cross with a spirit of devotion. His sermons on "The Suffering Saviour" reward the reader with insights sure to enrich heart and mind![17]

Samuel Zwemer, sometimes called the Apostle to Islam because of his missionary concern for the millions of the Muslim world, discerned that all the wealth and wonder of the gospel

15. Stuart Barton Babbage, *The Light of the Cross* (Grand Rapids: Zondervan, 1966).

16. Marcus Loane, *Life Through The Cross* (Grand Rapids: Zondervan, 1966).

17. F.W. Krummacher, *The Suffering Saviour* (reprinted, Chicago: Moody Press n.d.).

centers in the cross of Christ. His significant book, *The Glory of the Cross*, consists of meditations on the passion and death of our Lord.[18] It affirms the historicity of the crucifixion and the necessity of the atonement, in the face of their denial by Muslim and theological modernist alike. Zwemer rightly believed that only Christ crucified would draw all men to Himself, for it is under the shadow of His cross alone that any man shall ever find the rest and peace of the forgiveness of sins.

One of the outstanding preachers of the Free Church of Scotland was Hugh Martin. Among his many books are volumes on Jonah's character and mission, the doctrine of biblical inspiration, and the Headship of Christ over the Church. "The Shadow of Calvary," first published in 1875, has been reprinted several times since and still helps in preparation for the preaching of the cross today. He presents the story of redemption under three main headings: Gethsemane, The Arrest, and The Trial.

A monumental trilogy by Klaas Schilder of the Netherlands, translated into English by Henry Zylstra, deals with the sacred drama in three volumes: "Christ in His Suffering," "Christ on Trial," and "Christ Crucified."[19] Schilder constantly calls us to consider Jesus as prophet, priest, and king in the course of expounding the message of the cross. Commenting on the cry, "It is finished," Schilder writes: "The completion of His life-task filled Him with an infallible and hence irresistible sense of joy ... All that had definitely been given Him to do had been accomplished. He had in His historical life achieved everything that the Scriptures had indicated as His Messianic task. The eternal and the temporal, the counsel of God and the deed of Christ, are combined in this utterance of our Victor."[20]

---

18. Samuel Zwemer, *The Glory of the Cross* (London: Oliphants, 1954).

19. Klaas Schilder, *Christ in His Suffering* (1942), *Christ on Trial* (1945), *Christ Crucified* (1940); (Grand Rapids: Baker, reprinted 1978).

20. Schilder, *Christ Crucified*, p. 450.

In presenting the personalities and events of the passion story, use your imagination. Put yourself and your hearers right where it happened. But let your creativity be exercised within the bounds of what Scripture expressly records. Recognize and resist the temptation to consider the personalities and events in isolation, apart from their relationship to the redemptive suffering of Jesus Christ. Never forget that they are peripheral. He alone is central. There is a sense in which we, like the disciples on the Mount of Transfiguration, must ever lift up the eyes of our faith and see "no one except Jesus" (Matt. 17:8).

The epistles, of course, interpret the significance of our Lord's suffering and death. Their teaching, whether from the pen of John, Peter, or Paul, accords with that of the prophets and the gospels. They proclaim Him as the Saviour who died to pay the penalty for the sins of His people, and left us an example that we should follow in His steps. In addition to studying the Scriptures, and exegetical commentaries and expositions distinguished for faithfulness to the written Word of God, we will find it useful to consult evangelical formulations of the doctrine of the atonement by biblical theologians like A.A. Hodge, George Smeaton, and Leon Morris. Their writings are most helpful to everyone who wants to echo the apostolic preaching of the cross in pulpit ministry today.

In preaching His redemption, we must relate the history narrated in the gospels to its authentic doctrinal interpretation and authoritative ethical application as revealed in the Scriptures. Consider, for instance, a series of messages applying the truth of the cross to the various aspects of our lives:

Ephesians 4:31, 32, The Cross and Real Forgiveness
Ephesians 5:22-33, The Cross and Family Life
Philippians 2:5-8, The Cross and True Humility
I Corinthians 6:19, 20, The Cross and Total Commitment
II Corinthians 8:9, The Cross and Hearty Benevolence
II Corinthians 5:14, 15, The Cross and Christian Service
John 13:34, 35, The Cross and Brotherly Love

The Book of Hebrews, declaring the supremacy and ex-
cellency of Christ in revelation and redemption, deserves far
more attention than it usually receives as a source for
preaching in the Lenten season. It teaches us much regarding
the nature and consequences of sin, the meaning of priesthood,
altar, and sacrifice, the doctrine of substitution, the practice of
intercession, and the experience of cleansing. Surely we ought
to study that inspired message first written to Hebrew Christians and proclaim it to Jew and Gentile in our time. As long as
our race is affected by sin, and Christ is the only Saviour, we
need to hear what the Spirit is saying to us through this book.

A word about appropriate music related to the preaching of
the cross may be in order at this point. The message of
Gethsemane, Gabbatha, and Golgotha was never meant to be
wedded to music associated with night clubs and dance halls.
Gospel music worthy of the name is primarily a matter of message set to suitable melody. What really counts is the communication of the gospel, that the Son of God loved us and gave
Himself for us, calling forth the devout reponse of repentence
and faith.

Evangelical hymnology at its finest finds its focus in Christ
crucified. We need to return to this focal point rather than be
distracted by the dazzling wardrobes of groups and the plastic
smiles of performers whose choice of music leaves much to be
desired. In the service of praise, as in the preaching of the
Word, Christ alone must have the preeminence.

A medieval hymn, ascribed to Bernard of Clairvaux and set
to music harmonized by Johann Sebastian Bach, gives expression to the message of the cross with sublime simplicity. "O
Sacred Head, Now Wounded," is an excellent example of the
kind of hymn we should be singing in praise of our blessed
Redeemer.

Our hymnic heritage includes Palm Sunday selections such
as "All Glory, Laud, and Honour," as well as "Ride On! Ride On
in Majesty." On the theme of our Lord's agony, there is "Go to
Dark Gethsemane," while the story and significance of Calvary

are simply but powerfully recalled in "There Is a Green Hill Far Away." Through songs like "Beneath the Cross of Jesus" and "When I Survey the Wondrous Cross," we may well express the response of the heart to the sacrifice of redeeming love.

It is high time that we turned from the beat and sound of blues, jazz, and rock to the direction of music more appropriate to the message of the cross when remembering our Redeemer in His death.

Surely we ought to be glad for the redemption wrought by Jesus Christ on our behalf. We may, and must, rejoice in the Lord through whom we have the forgiveness of sins and peace with God. But let that joy be a reverent rejoicing in the presence of a crucified and risen Lord, rather than a show of superficial enthusiasm or sentimentality only remotely related to the reality of His sacrifice.

3

Christ Over Us

Celebrating His Coronation

The portrait of Christ presented in Scripture has line, form, color, perspective, and chiaroscuro—the interplay of light and shadow. We see the darkness of His humiliation and the brightness of His exaltation. Prophets and apostles portray Him in this way. Isaiah, for example, not only refers to the sufferings of the Servant of the Lord but also foretells His triumph. The obedient Servant shall be buried with honor and share the spoil of His victory with the strong (Isa. 53).

The apostle Peter mentions that our salvation is related to "the sufferings of Christ and the glories that would follow" (I Peter 1:11). After describing the descent of God's Equal to service and suffering, culminating in the death of the cross, Paul declares that God "exalted him to the highest place and gave him the name that is above every name, that at the name of Jesus every knee should bow, in heaven and on earth and under the earth, and every tongue confess that Jesus Christ is Lord, to the glory of God the Father" (Phil. 2:9-11).

Our Lord Jesus Christ personally interpreted the Old Testament Scriptures along these lines. He was aware of shadow and light, humiliation and exaltation. He knew that the Messiah had to suffer and then rise from the dead on the third day (Luke 24:44-46).

RESURRECTION

The writers of the New Testament are absolutely unanimous in affirming that Jesus Christ is alive. On the third day after His passion and death, He arose triumphant over death. His resurrection body bore the wounds of redeeming love in hands, feet, and side. The risen Lord was none other than the crucified Christ.

This historical reality is basic to Christian faith. It is the fact of His resurrection that sustains our faith in Him, and not our faith in Him that has fabricated the story of that first Easter. The fact of the resurrection created faith in the risen Lord. It transformed a group of discouraged, depressed, defeated disciples into bold witnesses for world evangelization. It serves to give us confidence and courage despite the grim reality of death.

Let us be clear on this: the New Testament speaks of the resurrection of Christ as an historical fact. It actually happened, just as His arrest, scourging, crucifixion, and death had actually happened. Jesus did not merely live on as a melancholy memory in the mind of His followers. They did not experience hallucinations, but encountered the risen Lord alive after His passion. How literally did they take His resurrection? As literally as a piece of broken bread on the table of a wayside inn on the road to Emmaus!

Jesus predicted not only His cross, but His resurrection as well. Repeatedly, Jesus warned the disciples that He would face betrayal, arrest, false accusation, and violent execution by an apostate hierarchy in conspiracy with illegitimate government. But He also assured them that on the third day He would rise again. And He did. (Matt. 16:21; Mark 8:31; John 2:19-22).

Jesus Christ was raised from the dead by the power of God the Father. His last word was neither with unscrupulous politicans like Pilate, nor sensual buffoons like Herod, nor evil priests like Caiaphas, but with God. That is why we glorify "the God of peace, who through the blood of the eternal covenant brought back from the dead our Lord Jesus, that great Shepherd of the sheep (Heb. 13:20).

Christ crucified was raised from the power of death by the might of the Holy Spirit. The very Spirit who wrought mightily when He was conceived in the womb of the Virgin Mary, demonstrated the dynamism of His deity in bringing Him forth from the womb of the earth and robbing the grave of its prey. As the Spirit resurrected Jesus from the dead on that third day, so He shall raise us from the dust at the last day (Rom. 8:9-11).

In the work of resurrection, Christ also had a part. Once He prophesied that if men were to destroy the temple of His body, He would raise it up on the third day (John 2:19-21). The Good Shepherd would not only give His life for the sheep sacrificially, but take it up again triumphantly. He declared: "No one takes it from me, but I lay it down of my own accord. I have authority to lay it down and authority to take it up again. This command I received from my Father" (John 10:18).

It is the resurrection of Christ from the dead that we commemorate and celebrate, not only on Easter but every Lord's Day. For it was on the first day of the week that our Lord and Saviour returned from the realm of the dead to bless His people with peace and joy (Matt. 28:1-10; Mark 16:1-8; Luke 24:1-42; John 20:1-23).

The resurrection of Christ assures Christians of their own blessed resurrection. It is because He lives that we too shall live. The victory of the Head guarantees the victory of all the members of His body. He holds the keys of death and hell. Let us not fear. Even man's last enemy shall be subdued at the last day by the sovereign power of the risen Lord (John 14:19; I Cor. 15:20-28, 50-58).

His resurrection also declares that God has vindicated the claims of Christ against the false accusations of ungodly men. They disputed His claim to deity, and denounced Him as a blasphemous impostor deserving of death. But God has proven all Christ's claims to be true by raising Him from the dead, and exalting Him to glory and honor (Acts 2:22-24; 3:13-15; 5:29-32). Surely "Christ was designated the Son of God when he rose from the dead, by an open exercise of true heavenly power, which was the power of the Spirit of holiness".[1]

If Jesus were still in the grave, what assurance would we have that the Father had acknowledged His death on the cross as a sufficient sacrifice for the sins of His people? But now Christ is risen from the dead. This signifies that His death has been accepted by God and we can be accepted by God through faith in Him. We have a living Saviour who was "delivered over to death for our sins and was raised to life for our justification" (Rom. 4:25). Thus did God give us "a solemn assurance that he is reconciled to guilty men" through faith in His risen Son.[2]

Because we believe that Christ is risen, we experience a "new and unanimous spirit of exhilaration, of overflowing joy, of indomitable confidence, of energetic enterprise." It all flows from the fact of the resurrection, "that awe-inspiring miracle on which the whole Christian faith depends".[3]

---

1. John Calvin, *Commentaries on the Epistle of Paul the Apostle to the Romans,* trans. and ed. John Owen (Edinburgh: Calvin Translation Society, 1849) p. 46 (on Rom. 1:4).

2. John Dick, *Lectures on Theology,* 2 vols. (New York: Robert Carter & Brothers, 1851) II:103.

3. Paul Claudel, *I Believe in God* (New York: Holt, Rinehart & Winston, 1961) pp. 140, 141.

ASCENSION

The New Testament tells us that after His resurrection, our Lord met with His disciples on many occasions and taught them truths regarding the Kingdom of God. He also commissioned them to go into all the world and make disciples out of every nation. He did not authorize cultural aggression or ecclesiastical imperialism, but the making of disciples through the preaching of the gospel and the works of compassion (Matt. 28:18-20; Luke 24:45-47; John 20:21; Acts 1:8). And then, forty days after His resurrection, Jesus ascended into heaven (Acts 1:9-11).

The ascension of our Lord is viewed critically by those who doubt or deny the inspiration and authority of the biblical narrative. This comes as no surprise. What is surprising, however, is the usual neglect of this wonderful reality in conservative, fundamental, and evangelical circles. One hears much about Christ coming into the world to save sinners. One is familiar with His death and resurrection and is encouraged to look with longing eyes for His return. All this is good. But where is the due emphasis deserved by the wonderful fact of the ascension in the proclamation and life of the Church today?

When Jesus Christ ascended to heaven before the wondering eyes of His disciples on the Mount of Olives, He demonstrated that His redemptive work on earth had been accomplished and now He was going back to the Father in heaven. He went upward as One who had faithfully accomplished His mission on earth, met the enemy and defeated Satan, and now was entitled to a conqueror's welcome as the hero of redemption (Ps. 68:18; Eph. 4:8; Ps. 24:7-10).

The ascension, like the resurrection, had been predicted by Jesus. Even as He stood in the lengthening shadow of the cross, He prophesied about moving upward to the place of majesty and authority at the Father's right hand in heaven (Mark 14:62). Forty days after Easter, that prophecy became history (Luke 24:50-53). Henceforth, the apostolic preaching would make repeated reference to the reality of the ascended Christ.

Peter did this at Pentecost, in the temple area, and before the rulers of the Jews. Stephen the martyr, enduring the violence of vicious men, lifted up his eyes to see the ascended Lord. And so must we, for it is from heaven that the Lord Jesus shall some day return to judge the living and the dead.

Christians demonstrate the reality of their conversion not merely by turning from idols to serve the living God, but also by looking for the return of God's Son from heaven—the very same Jesus whose death delivered them from wrath, the Christ who rose again from the dead (I Thess. 1:9, 10). More than that, we are to be drawn heavenward in thought and aspiration and affection, because Jesus Christ has ascended into heaven (Col. 3:1-4). Are we attracted by Him? Such concentration is the real secret of consecration.

It is high time that we renewed our emphasis on the ascension of Jesus Christ and recognized its tremendous implications for Him and all His people. "The greatest victory of God," said Calvin, "took place when Christ, having overcome sin, conquered death, and put Satan to flight, was lifted up to heaven in majesty, that he might reign gloriously over the church." Let us focus the eyes of our faith, hope, and love on Him who "ascended to the right hand of the Father, to bring to subjection all principalities and dominations, and then to become in eternity the defender and protector of the church".[4]

SESSION

What is our Lord doing in heaven? Calvin remarks "When we say that Christ is in heaven, we must not imagine that he is somewhere among the cosmic spheres, counting the stars! Heaven means a place far beyond all the spheres, destined for the Son of God after his resurrection".[5] There our ascended Lord continues His messianic work as prophet, priest, and king.

---

4. Calvin, *Commentaries on the Epistles of Paul to the Galatians and Ephesians*, trans. William Pringle (Edinburgh: Calvin Translation Society, 1854) p. 272 (on Eph. 4:8).

5. Ibid, p. 275 (on Eph. 4:10).

The session of Jesus Christ in heaven is marked by His continuing activity as our infallible prophet. He has not, because of His ascension, ceased to communicate to us the will of God for our salvation. He tells us what a man ought to believe and shows us the right pattern of behavior by means of His Word and Spirit. Indeed, the Spirit who inspired the sacred writings of the Old and New Testaments now opens our minds to understanding so that we may trust and obey to the glory of God.

Let us recall the promises of our Lord to His people. Did He not promise to pray that they might receive the Spirit of truth to be with them forever? Has He not said that the Spirit of truth will testify about Him, so that we will perceive the meaning of His unique person and saving work? The Spirit, according to the express pledge of Christ, was to come as the Spirit of truth to guide the disciples into all truth. He would not speak on His own, but glorify Christ by making known to us the things concerning our Lord and Saviour revealed in the Scriptures (John 14:16; 15:26; 16:13). This promise was kept at Pentecost when the Lord Jesus had ascended to heaven and poured out the Spirit on His praying people (John 7:37-39; Acts 2:33).

The Christ who is seated at God's right hand continues to serve as our merciful high priest. The sacrificial aspect of His priestly work was accomplished once and for all when He gave Himself on the altar of Calvary to atone for the sins of His people (John 19:30; Heb. 1:3; 9:12). But now, risen from the dead, ascended into heaven, He still bears us in His heart and intercedes for us. He presents the merits of that unique sacrifice in the heavenly sanctuary, and so answers all Satan's accusations against us (Rom. 8:33, 34). Despite our daily failings, we may experience peace of conscience by confessing our sins and trusting in Him as our advocate (I John 1:9; 2:1). Through Him who is perfect in His righteousness, we gain access to the throne of grace (Heb. 4:14-16; John 14:6). Because of Him who introduces all penitent believers to the Father, we find acceptance for our persons, prayers, and praises (Eph. 1:6; Heb. 13:15). Surely, "Christ the Intercessor is Christ the Redeemer actually carrying out in glory that work of love" whose foundations were laid on the earth[6]

The ascended Christ is now enthroned as King, and to the reality of His royalty the Holy Spirit bears clear witness in the Scriptures. Recall what the apostle Peter says on this theme. He declares that the crucified Christ is now risen from the dead and exalted to the place of supreme authority and power. From thence has the Lord Jesus sent the gift of the Spirit. Eventually, every enemy shall be subdued to His sovereignty (Acts 2:33-36). The cross, resurrection, and ascension have been followed by coronation. Christ is "at God's right hand — with angels, authorities and powers in submission to him" (I Peter 3:22).

The apostle Paul is also led by the Spirit to testify of the present kingship of Christ. He proclaims Jesus as Lord, exalted to highest honor and glory after His faithful obedience and the endurance of the cross (Phil. 2:6-11). Christ is seated at God's right hand "in the heavenly realms, far above all rule and authority, power and dominion, and every title that can be given, not only in the present age but also in the one to come ... God placed all things under his feet and appointed him to be head over everything for the Church" (Eph. 1:20-22). The conquering Christ has shared the spoils of His victory over death and hell, bestowing apostles, prophets, evangelists, pastors and teachers upon His people. Why? So that they might, through these ministries, be prepared for works of service and arrive at last to spiritual maturity (Eph. 4:7-16).

The apostle John points us to Jesus Christ, the Lamb once sacrificed and now enthroned, crowned with many crowns. He is King of kings and Lord of lords, worthy of worship (Rev. 19:16). The angels encircling the throne join with the elders and the living creatures, singing: "Worthy is the Lamb, who was slain to receive power and wealth and wisdom and

6. James Denney, *Studies in Theology* (London: Hodder & Stoughton, 1898), p. 169.

strength and honor and glory and praise!" And every creature in the entire universe unites in doxology: "To him who sits on the throne and to the Lamb be praise and honor and glory and power, for ever and ever!" (Rev. 5:12, 13).

Although we do not see all things yet subject to the glorious sovereignty of our Saviour, He is even now to be acknowledged as the One who possesses "all authority in heaven and on earth." We are, therefore, authorized to "go and make disciples of all nations, baptizing them in the name of the Father and of the Son and of the Holy Spirit," teaching them to obey everything He has commanded us (Matt. 28;18, 19). Surely this royal Messiah deserves our "profound reverence and prompt obedience".[7]

REVELATION

Some day, in the providence of God, this exalted Lord Jesus Christ shall return. The promise of His coming was definitely given at the time of His departure. Ascension and advent are inseparably linked in these words, first spoken to the disciples on the Mount of Olives: "Men of Galilee, why do you stand here looking into the sky? This same Jesus, who has been taken from you into heaven, will come back in the same way as you have seen him go into heaven" (Acts 1:11).

There are several words used in the Greek New Testament to describe the return of our exalted Lord. One is "parousia," or presence, which was an official term for the visit of a high-ranking person to a province, adopted by the apostles to express the advent of Christ in glory to judge the world at the end of this age (Matt. 24:3; I Cor. 1:8; II Thess. 2:8; II Peter 3:4). Another word is "epiphaneia," appearing, which refers not only to our Lord's first advent in grace but His return in glory (Titus 2:11, 13). Now hidden from our eyes, He shall manifest Himself by personal appearance at the last day. The Bible also speaks of the "apokalupsis", or revelation of Jesus Christ. This

---

7. Dick, *Lectures*, II:120.

word, of course, is transliterated as "apocalypse." It points to
the disclosure of truth (Rom. 16:25; Eph. 1:17), and particularly
of the unveiling of Christ, in all His sovereignty and splendor
when He comes again (I Peter 1:7, 13; 4:13; II Thess. 1:7).

On the basis of what the Bible says, we hold fast to our
blessed hope — the promise of His coming. "He who was unjust-
ly judged and condemned by wicked men, shall come again at
the last day in great power, and in the full manifestation of his
own glory, and of his Father's, with all his holy angels, with a
shout, with the voice of the archangel, and with the trumpet of
God, to judge the world in righteousness".[8]

We are not given this promise to promote panic or stimulate
speculation. We are assured of His advent so that our repentance, diligence, and vigilance may be encouraged. Hope is
meant to nurture holiness. Biblical prophecy is a powerful incentive to the practice of godliness. Scriptural eschatology
should result in scriptural ethics, not irresponsible escapism.

While we are not told the time of the advent of our exalted
Lord, we do find clues in biblical revelation as to the events
related to His coming. For example, there shall be the resurrection of the blessed dead and the transformation of believers
yet alive on the earth when He returns (I Thess. 4:13-18). Our
conformity to His glorious resurrection body, beyond the reach
of deformity, debility, disease, or death, awaits His advent
(Phil. 3:20). So does the judgment of the world in righteousness.
At that day shall there be an open distribution of rewards and
punishments, demonstrating the equity and finality of our
Lord's royal authority (John 5:21-29; Rev. 20:11-15). Surely this
should move sinners to repentance (Acts 17:30, 31), and servants to obedience (II Tim. 4:1-5). Let us learn to reckon real-
istically with the present fact and future revelation of Christ
over us.

8. Westminster Larger Catechism, in *A Harmony of the Westminster
Presbyterian Standards*, compiled by J.B. Green (Richmond: John Knox Press,
1965) Q. 56 (p. 62).

CELEBRATING HIS CORONATION

Jesus Christ lives now on the throne of the universe. Angels, principalities, and powers have been put under Him. Like the writers of the New Testament, we must take His glorious sovereignty seriously, and proclaim it with sacred joy.

The supremacy of Christ is absolute and universal. Scripture plainly and powerfully affirms this. But how shall we celebrate the coronation of our King through preaching? We believe that He lives and reigns in grace, but how shall we best declare this glorious truth and win others to His crown and kingdom?

Let us begin where each of the four canonical gospels ends — with the resurrection of Jesus Christ from the dead. Expound the message of His victory over death. The salvation and comfort of people who must pass through the valley of the shadow of death demands a clear presentation of the gospel of the resurrection.

The earliest and most reliable manuscripts of Mark's gospel, according to some scholars, give us grounds for suppposing that it came to an abrupt close at 16:8. They have even suggested that the writer was in the middle of describing how the news of the resurrection had produced a sense of amazement and reverential fear, when his writing was suddenly interrupted by enemies of the faith who put him under arrest.

In Matthew's much fuller account, the following emphases are included:

28:1-7, the announcement of the resurrection of Jesus the crucified,

28:8-10, the appearance of the risen Lord, and the adoration of those who then became the first ambassadors of the resurrection news,

After a parenthetical reference to the bribery of some soldiers to explain away the missing body of Jesus (28:11-15), the main line of the narrative continues:

28:16-20, the adoration of His person, affirmation of His power, announcement of His purpose, and assurance of His presence,

Luke's account contains some material not found in Matthew or Mark. He shows us the risen Christ comforting, correcting, and commissioning His people.

24:1-12, the Lord is risen from the dead, fulfilling the prophecies He had personally and repeatedly made.

24:13-35, the risen Saviour meets discouraged disciples on the way to Emmaus, and gradually brings them to an awareness of His identity and triumph through the explanation of messianic promises and the breaking of bread at eventide.

24:36-49, Christ brings His people peace, reassuring them of His victory over death. He shares with them a missionary purpose: that of inviting men everywhere to experience the remission of sins on the condition of repentance, and gives the disciples a promise regarding the power of the Spirit who will enable them to serve as the Lord's witnesses to all nations.

Luke notes how the Lord Jesus interpreted the Old Testament's Law, Prophets, and Psalms with reference to His own sufferings and consequent glory. Let us understand the Scriptures in this very way, christologically, as we preach the incarnate Word from the written Word.

John devotes the last two chapters of his gospel to a presentation of the good news of the resurrection:

20:1-9, in which the affection of Mary Magdalene for the missing Master, the association of Peter and John in their quest for Christ, and the apprehension of these disciples due to their misunderstanding of the Scriptures, are portrayed.

20:10-18, where we read of the consolation, correction, and commission of Mary Magdalene by the risen Lord in a memorable encounter.

20:19-23, reminiscent of Luke 24:36-49, with a word of peace (gloom yields to confidence and joy when we know that He is risen); a word of purpose (sent by the Father, the Son now sends His people to the ends of the earth bearing a message of forgiveness); a word of power (as the Creator breathed life into Adam, so Christ bestows the vitality of the Spirit to those who must serve Him in the world).

20:24-31, where John indicates the sources of doubt (absence from the fellowship when Christ is present, refusal to accept the testimony of credible witnesses); the secret of certainty (a personal encounter with the risen Lord revealed to us in the Scriptures).

21:1-14, in which failure is transformed as we obey the orders of the living Lord, and fellowship is experience with the Christ of the resurrection.

21:15-25, where Christ claims our love, and love qualifies us for the fulfillment of duty, and devotion to duty may involve a destiny of suffering.

In expounding the Johannine material, you will have occasion to relate something of the stories involving Peter, John, Mary Magdalene, and Thomas, as these are given in the earlier chapters of the gospel. But however interesting such character studies may be, keep the Christ of the resurrection at the center of your proclamation. Celebrate His triumph over death, and make plain the glorious consequences of that victory for all His people everywhere.

Never forget that the basis for our Easter faith is not feeling but fact — the actual, historical, bodily resurrection of the crucified from the dead. Sometime expound the fifteenth chapter of I Corinthians during the weeks following Easter. Here the event and its importance are masterfully presented by the apostle Paul. When sects teaching strange doctrines about death and the after-life abound and the ensuing confusion is complicated by the scoffing of sceptics within and without the visible Church, it must certainly be the responsibility of every pastor/teacher among God's people to declare and apply the message of this chapter through systematic and relevant exposition. In unfolding the apostolic teaching here presented, you might proceed along these lines:

15:1-11, in which we are given gospel content (redemption and resurrection); and gospel communication (received from the Lord, preached by the apostles, believed by the Corinthians).

15:12-19, where we are confronted with the consequences for the integrity of our preaching, the reality of our salvation, and the certainty of our hope, if Christ did not rise from the dead on that third day after His passion.

15:20-28, emphasizing the primacy of Christ, a parellelism with Adam, and the promise of victory.

15:29-34, which mentions the enigmatic matter of baptism for the dead, and goes on to deal with our own dying to sin and rising to righteousness in fellowship with the living Lord.

15:35-49, descriptive of the resurrection process, and the resurrection body.

15:50-58, vibrant with the hope of universal transformation, joyful anticipation, and practical exhortation.

What about the ascension of our Lord? This, too, must be presented as an historical event of great significance. The narratives in Luke 24:50-53 and Acts 1:9-11 provide us with a definite basis for preaching on the subject. Indeed, the entire Book of Acts (which might also be called II Luke) is an unfolding of the significance of the Redeemer's ascension. The crucified and risen Lord is now in heaven, enthroned in majesty, entitled to supreme authority, exercising supernatural power at God's right hand. From thence He had poured out the gift of the Spirit and empowered the Church to continue His unfinished work in the world.

Henry Barclay Swete, once professor of divinity at Cambridge, wrote: "Few things are more important than that Christian people should learn to realize the fact of our Lord's risen and ascended life, and its relation to their own lives and hopes.[9] We can help meet this need by faithfully expounding the book of the Acts of the Apostles.

Because of the length of the Book of Acts, it is not advisable to present the entire run of twenty-eight chapters in a course of sermons that might take too many months. It seems wiser to study the structure of Acts, note the main divisions, and then present one section each year following the Easter-Ascension period until the whole has been expounded.

---

9. H.B. Swete, *The Appearances of our Lord After the Passion* (London: Macmillan, 1908) p. vii.

Concentrate on the Christ whom those Spirit-filled messengers proclaimed, noting His person and work, as well as prophecy and fulfillment. Note also a way in which the missioners varied their approach, depending on their audience. Peter's procedure on the day of Pentecost in Jerusalem was followed by Paul's in the synagogue at Pisidian Antioch, but Paul took a different line in presenting the gospel to the pagans of Lystra and the philosophers of Athens. We must begin where our hearers are, and then be led by the Spirit to lead them to Christ.

In studying the apostolic work of evangelization, notice the principles and practices that are still valid and applicable for the spread of the gospel within and across cultures today. Nor have the reactions to the presentation of Christ changed. People still respond with hostility, indifference, procrastination, doubt, or commitment to our Lord and Saviour.

The celebration of His coronation will inevitably mean expounding the great theme of the letter to the Hebrews: the unique and surpassing excellence of Jesus Christ, the Son of God. Climax of the process of revelation, finisher of the work of redemption, indispensable to the experience of reconciliation, He is now exalted as prophet, priest, and king at God's right hand:

1:1-4, see the Christ who reveals (the God who spoke through the prophets in the past has in these last days spoken to us in His Son); redeems (radiance of the divine glory, sustainer of the universe He has made, Christ has provided purification for sins through the sacrifice of Himself); reigns (having accomplished redemption, He is enthroned in the place of heavenly majesty).

2:14-18, behold Christ as our merciful and faithful high priest; He identified with us in His incarnation, and made atonement for us at the cross; though He is exalted far above us in heavenly glory, we can be sure He understands and cares.

4:14-16, contemplate the Christ who is no stranger to our weaknesses, but sympathizes with us and opens the way for us to draw near to the very heart of God for grace to help us in time of need.

7:23-28, consider Him who is not mortal and sinful as other priests have been; He is sinless and lives for ever; the benefits of His sacrifice continue to be applied to His people since He makes constant intercession on their behalf in God's presence.

10:19-22, know that since Christ is the way to the Father, all who approach God through Him gain access and enjoy fellowship with the Holy One; be ever confident of the intercession of this royal Redeemer.

12:1-2, look unto Jesus, the supreme example of endurance through the valley of humiliation to the height of exaltation, as you run the race set before you.

13:20-21, draw encouragement from the fact that the God of peace has brought again from the dead our Lord Jesus Christ, the great shepherd of the flock; and that He can equip us with everything good for the doing of His will, working in us what is pleasing to Him.

The season following Easter and the Ascension is a most appropriate time to expound the New Testament epistles with their focus on the risen, reigning Lord. Think, for example, of the Philippian letter and its great emphasis on the humiliation/exaltation of Christ as the pattern for every believer (2:5-11). Or, the Colossian correspondence, with its claim concerning the preeminence of Christ (1:15-20), and call to identification with Christ in His death, resurrection, and return (3:1-4). The Ephesian epistle also emphasizes the majesty of Him whom God has raised from the dead and exalted to the place of supreme power (1:15-23; 4:7-16).

Although the Lord's return is touched on when the message of Advent is presented, it finds much greater prominence in the course of celebrating His coronation. He is now King of kings and Lord of lords. He will not suddenly become Lord and King at His coming, but at that time the full extent of His royalty shall be finally revealed. Christ will come again at the appointed moment to judge the world in righteousness. Reward and retribution will be publicly distributed by Him in the display of His royal authority. The judgment passed on each person at the termination of his life on earth will be solemnly ratified by Christ at the end of the world.

This is as good a point as any at which to make some comments on biblical prophecy. Every prophetic passage ought to be taken in its context and not abused as a pretext to support questionable theories about the future. We should, moreover, ask ourselves if the prophecy has already been fulfilled (as in the case of the return of Israel from the exile to the land of promise, or the birth of the Messiah in Bethlehem, or the outpouring of the Spirit at Pentecost as predicted by Joel). Is the prophecy one still being fulfilled, or is it awaiting its fulfillment? How does it relate to the saving and judging work of our sovereign God? We must also be aware of the intensely practical purpose of biblical prophecy. It is never given to stimulate speculation, but to stir repentance, encourage obedience, sharpen vigilance, strengthen endurance, and sustain confidence.

In preaching on the return of Christ, our Judge and King, let the accent fall on His supreme majesty and glorious triumph, rather than on the beast, the dragon, the harlot, and the antichrist. Unless we see Christ as preeminent, we will miss the main point of Scripture in general and the Book of Revelation in particular.

The Revelation is primarily about Him—the Lamb once slain, the Lion who is strong, the Christ of the cross, now crowned with many crowns. He alone is Head of the Church and Lord of history, Judge of the living and the dead.

When presenting the opening chapters of this book, for example, you will want to deal with what they reveal about Jesus Christ as well as consider His evaluation of the Church. The many titles ascribed to Him, such as "the faithful witness, the firstborn from the dead, and the ruler of the kings of the earth" (Rev. 1:5), are most significant. So are His penetrating insights regarding the state of the churches. He sees their activity, orthodoxy and suffering. He is aware of their declension from first love, their dilution of doctrine, and their drift from biblical morality. He probes and prescribes, as the Great Physician who deeply desires the renewal of the spiritual vitality of His people. The relevant exposition of our Lord's letters to the seven churches of the Apocalypse will enable us to hear what the Spirit is saying to the churches in our time and produce revival whenever we are ready to repent, believe, and obey.

What about the millennial question? Honesty leads us to admit that not all evangelicals share the same eschatological view. There are varieties of interpretations held by persons equally committed to the inspiration of Scripture and the return of the Lord. The millennium may be described as a thousand-year period of peace over which Christians fight!

Devout disciples have held views known as postmillennial, premillennial, or amillennial. Simply put, the postmillennial doctrine is that the kingdom of Christ is now being advanced through missions and the leavening influence of Christianity on the world. The return of Christ is supposed to come after the kingdom's emergence.

The premillennial teaching is that the kingdom will not begin before the return of Christ. In the first phase of prophetic fulfillment, Christ comes for His people and takes them out of this world. Will the rapture happen before, during, or after the tribulation? Premillennialists are not unanimous as to the sequence of these events. In the second phase, Christ will return with His people to this earth, defeat the antichrist, and establish a thousand year rule of unprecedented blessing — to be followed by a conflict with Satan, the resurrection of the wicked, and the judgment at the great white throne.

The amillennial view is that the thousand year kingdom (mentioned in Revelation 20) is to be interpreted symbolically. It stands for the present kingship of Him who is Lord. While postmillennialists say that the world is getting better, and premillennialists deplore worsening trends, amillennialists say that both the wheat and the tares are growing along together and will be separated with finality only at the end when Christ returns to judgment.

The proclamation of Christ's kingship and the message of His kingdom should be based on Scripture, not speculation. Let us avoid the arrogance of presuming to know more about the precise fulfillment of every prophecy than our Lord and His apostles. We must never lose sight of the fact that not every Christian shares the same prophetic viewpoint. None of us has all the answers concerning the future. Does this mean that we ought never to preach on prophecy? Of course not. We are called to declare the whole counsel of God, and that includes prophecy. But let us be careful in our preparation, guarded in our interpretation, and practical in our application.

For the serial exposition of the Scriptures closely relating evangelism, ethics, and eschatology, the New Testament epistles offer an abundance of homiletical resources. Why not present the Thessalonian letters, so filled with the Christian hope centered in the return of God's Son from heaven, yet so mindful of Christian responsibility in the world while awaiting His advent?

Consider the letter to Jude with its sharp warning against apostasy, and clear call to contend earnestly for the faith while looking for the appearing of the Lord. Or II Peter, in which the promise of His coming and the glorious prospect of the renewal of the universe are related to the ethical imperative. In preaching of biblical prophecy, let nothing distract you from the practical presentation of the truth of God. Point to Christ, who is our hope, and call people to prepare for His return through repentance and faith. Above all, celebrate the glory of Him whose right to reign has been clearly confirmed by the Father as the due reward of an accomplished redemption. "Worthy is the Lamb, who was slain, to receive power and wealth and wisdom and strength and honor and glory and praise!" (Rev. 5:12).

The resources of Christian hymnology on the theme of Christ's exaltation are rich indeed. Let us draw on them, choosing hymns in praise of Him who accomplished redemption, defeated death, subdued Satan, and reigns in glory.

Hymns such as "Christ the Lord Is Risen Today," "The Strife Is O'er, the Battle Won," "Come Ye Faithful, Raise the Strain," and "Thine Be the Glory, Risen, Conquering Son," are vibrant with the victory of Him who has overcome death and brought life and immortality to light.

Our Lord's ascension to the right hand of the majesty of God in heaven and His ministry there, are the themes of praise selections like "The Head that Once was Crowned with Thorns," "Crown Him with Many Crowns," "Jesus Shall Reign," "Look Ye Saints, the Sight Is Glorious," and "Where High the Heavenly Temple Stands." Notable among the hymns announcing His return are "Thou Art Coming, O My Saviour" and "Rejoice, the Lord Is King."

Whether spoken or sung, let the message of the exaltation of Jesus Christ be faithfully presented and clearly heard. In times when conflicting ideologies clamor for the allegiance of hearts and minds, we must present the claims of this Redeemer King and win the loyalties of men and women to the banner of His cross and crown.

4

Christ Within Us

Preparing His Habitation

The Christ of the cradle, cross, and crown will someday return in power and glory to judge the world in righteousness. But even now we can experience the presence of the Lord by the Spirit sent from heaven to dwell within us.

Who is this Holy Spirit? It goes without saying that by the Spirit of Christ we do not mean merely "a Christian attitude" but the third person of the Trinity. Coming to us from the Father and the Son, equal with them in His being, power, and glory, the Spirit is deserving of our faith, love, obedience, and adoration. His personality and deity are plainly affirmed in Holy Scripture.

As the Lord and Giver of life, He is omnipresent. All good thoughts, pure desires, and holy counsels come from Him. The Spirit restrains the effects of sin so that we can exist in this evil world. As He moved the holy prophets to proclaim the message of God and caused the sacred writings to be produced for our guidance in matters of creed and conduct, so He enables us to understand the truth and empowers us to obey it. To refuse the Spirit who speaks in the Scriptures, whether through disbelief or disobedience, is to resist God and incur His displeasure.

INDIVIDUALLY

The Spirit comes to dwell in the individual believer as Christ's personal representative. The man who follows mere natural instincts does not have the Spirit. But unless we are indwelt and directed by the Spirit of Christ, we cannot consider ourselves Christians (Jude 19; Rom. 8:9).

We should never forget that the Spirit comes to reside in us and preside over us on behalf of the Lord Jesus Christ. The Corinthians needed to be reminded of this. On one occasion, Paul asked, "Do you not know that your body is a temple of the Holy Spirit, who is in you, whom you have received from God? You are not your own; you were bought at a price. Therefore honor God with your body" (I Cor. 6:19, 20).

The redemption accomplished by Christ is applied by the Spirit of Christ to the people of Christ as He dwells within them individually. The Spirit who works within us produces new life. He regenerates us. By nature, we are blind, bound, and born in sin. As Jesus told Nicodemus, the unregenerate man cannot see the kingdom of God. He does not perceive spiritual truths, nor can he take the necessary steps on his own to enter the kingdom of God. He inherits sinful humanity just as he has inherited a sinful nature from those who generated him. There is only one way out — regeneration by the power of the Holy Spirit. In the process of making me a new person, the Spirit uses the Scriptures. Whenever and however I come alive in Christ, it is solely because of the Spirit's work within me, and not due to making resolutions or performing rituals. (John 3:1-8; I Peter 1:22-25; James 1:17; Ezek. 36:25-27).

The Spirit of regeneration also convicts of sin, according to Christ's promise. As the divine attorney for the prosecution,

He sets forth the evidence of our doubt, disbelief, and disobedience. He confronts us with the law of God, broken by our sin, and exposes our guilt in His sight, so that we are reduced to repentance. We experience contrition and express our personal confession because of the work of the Spirit of Christ within our hearts (Zech. 12:10; John 16:8-11). Thanks be to God for the ministry of the Spirit who comes "convincing of sin, breaking the heart with godly sorrow, laying the soul low in the dust of self-abasement and self-condemnation before God, then leading it to the atoning blood of Jesus and speaking pardon and peace to the conscience".[1]

Faith, like repentance, is an evidence of the Spirit's ministry within. He persuades us to put our trust in Jesus Christ, to receive Him as He is freely offered to us in the gospel, and to rely on Him alone for our salvation (II Cor. 4:13; Acts 16:31; I Cor. 12:3). We would never know the benefit of Christ's saving work for us apart from His Spirit's grace within us. It is the Spirit who produces "a profound understanding of one's own lost condition, an illumination of the deadened conscience which causes a Copernican revolution in one's attitude toward the world and toward God," so indispensable to our salvation?[2]

The Spirit quickens and sustains our new life in fellowship with the living Lord of glory so that His vitality fills our being and flows out from us to others in rich blessing (John 7:37-39; 15:1-8).

It is the Spirit within who enlightens our minds. He dispels the darkness and gives us understanding. The things of God are dismissed as nonsense by the unregenerate mind. But when the Spirit brings the truth of Scripture to light and gives us eyes to perceive, we see ourselves in relationship to Christ as Saviour and Lord (John 14:16, 17; 26; 16:13, 14; Eph. 1:17, 18; I Cor. 2:9-16).

---

1. Octavius Winslow, *The Work of the Holy Spirit*, 1843, (Reprint, London: Banner of Truth Trust, 1961) p. 97.

2. J. Gresham Machen, *Christianity and Liberalism*, 1923, (Grand Rapids: Eerdman, n.d.) p. 106.

Christ's vicar is the agent of sanctification. He enables us to mortify the old egocentric nature inherited from Adam and nurtured by ourselves. The Spirit not only provides powerful help in struggling against "the flesh," but produces in us the character of Christ (Rom. 8:13; Gal. 5:16-24). The sanctifying work of this "great inhabitant of the regenerate heart" is indispensable to our progress in godliness. This indwelling "underlies all the Christian's holiness and growth, all his conformity to the divine image and final perseverance".[3]

Having begun a good work in us, the Spirit will bring it to perfection at the last. For His presence in us is the seal or mark of God's ownership. He will not abandon those who belong to Him. What he commences in grace shall be consummated in glory (Eph. 1:13; 4:30; II Cor. 1:22).

We must remember that the proof of the Spirit's presence within us is not superficial, transitory, or fanatical excitement, but ethical behavior conforming to the standard set forth in Scripture. The Spirit of Christ is the Spirit of holiness, as well as of truth and power. He uses the truth and exercises His power to produce purity. We must also bear in mind the fact that the Spirit is devoted to the glory of Christ. All His work within us finds its focus in Christ. Whatever leads us to trust Christ and obey Him is of the Spirit of God. Whatever blurs or mars His image in us can never be justified — much less sanctified, or glorified!

Beyond all doubt or dispute, "the rule of sanctification is the word of God . . . this is the rule according to which the Spirit works, forming in us those dispositions which it promises or requires, and the rule according to which we should work in the whole course of our Christian profession".[4] To neglect the Bible in favor of some human tradition or innovation, to depreciate Scripture by seeking some other "revelation" from

---

3. George Smeaton, *The Doctrine of the Holy Spirit*, 1882, (Reprint, London: Banner of Truth Trust, 1958) pp. 210, 211.

4. John Dick, *Lectures on Theology*, 2 vols. (New York: Robert Carter & Brothers, 1851) II:247.

the Spirit, is to grieve Him who inspired the sacred writings and hinder our growth in godliness.

It is the Spirit who completes Christ's reconciling work. As Christ died to remove estrangement and enmity, so the Spirit within assures us that the way back is clear. He encourages us to use the open access that is shown us in the gospel, and encourages us to speak with the Almighty on the most affectionate terms. The Spirit tells us that we belong to God's family and are destined to enjoy the riches of an everlasting inheritance (Eph. 2:14-18; Rom. 8:14-17; 8:26, 27; Gal. 4:4-7).

Do we know "the comfort, holiness, and filial walk of the believer who is conscious that he is a temple of the Holy Ghost"?[5] No idols must desecrate the sanctuary consecrated to His presence within. We must be completely and uniquely open to Him who comes with "all His regenerating, sanctifying, sealing, and comforting influence",[6] else we shall fail to experience "righteousness, peace and joy in the Holy Spirit" (Rom. 14:17).

Our Lord once promised, "Whoever has my commands and obeys them, he is the one who loves me. He who loves me will be loved by my Father, and I, too, will love him and show myself to him ... If anyone loves me, he will obey my teaching. My father will love him, and will come to him, and make our home with him" (John 14:21, 23). This promise has been kept. The Spirit has been sent to dwell with Christ's people and live within each disciple. The Spirit-filled believer experiences the Spirit "transforming history into song, chaos into melody, and incoherence into assent." He confesses, "All that the Father has wrought in me, all that He has devised to let me be His son and to be born into the understanding of Him, the how and why, the Spirit is there to explain it all, to instill it in me, to impart it to my soul".[7]

---

5. Winslow, *Holy Spirit*, p. 88.

6. Ibid, p. 88.

7. Paul Claudel, *I Believe in God* (New York: Holt, Rinehart & Winston, 1961) pp. 161, 167.

SOCIALLY

The dynamic presence of Christ is experienced not only by the individual disciple, but also by the community of believers. His Spirit "insists on lodging permanently within us, within each of us, and within us as a Church".[8]

If the individual is to consider himself as a shrine of the Spirit, so must the Church. The indwelling of the Holy Spirit is not a private, personal affair but involves the whole fellowship of faith. In the Scriptures the very existence of the Church is due to the creative activity of the Spirit who regenerates individuals and relates them both to Christ and one another. According to the Bible, "not only the life of the Church but its continuing growth, its renewal, and the great hope by which it is sustained are ascribed to the presence and power of the Holy Spirit".[9]

Christ has promised to be in the midst of His people when they gather together by His authority to do His work. He has pledged Himself to be with them always as they go forth to fulfill the great commission. This promise He keeps by the presence and power of the Spirit in the Church.

The true Church is composed of Christ plus His people. He builds His temple with stones drawn from the quarries of countless countries. Through evangelization and edification, this sanctuary is built in fulfillment of God's design. Resting on the firm "foundation of the apostles and prophets, with Christ Jesus himself as the chief cornerstone, the whole building is joined together and rises to become a holy temple in the Lord . . . a dwelling in which God lives by his Spirit" (Eph. 2:20-22).

Paul asks, "Don't you know that you yourselves are God's temple and that God's Spirit lives in you? If anyone destroys God's temple, God will destroy him; for God's temple is sacred,

8. T. F. Torrance, *When Christ Comes and Comes Again,* (Grand Rapids: Eerdmans, 1957) p. 109.

9. G. S. Hendry, *The Westminster Confession for Today,* (London: SCM Press, 1960) p. 120.

and you are that temple" (I Cor. 3:16, 17). How is God's temple destroyed? By heresy, a deadly departure from the historic faith of the gospel revealed in the Scriptures, and by schism, a loveless division between fellow believers due to pride. Heresy and schism are taken most seriously by God and threatened with severe punishment because He loves the Church indwelt by the Spirit of His Son.

Consider the work of the Spirit within the society of Jesus. He unites all believers in Christ and to each other so that they form one body together. Thus the apostle Paul remarked, "For we were all baptized by one Spirit into one body — whether Jews or Greeks, slave or free — and we were all given the one Spirit to drink" (I Cor. 12:13). That is why we must be humble, gentle, patient, forbearing, and loving, within the fellowship. We are under obligation to "keep the unity of the Spirit through the bond of peace," remembering that "there is one body and one Spirit" (Eph. 4:2-4).

When the Spirit of Christ dwells within the community of truth and love, real spiritual life is experienced. The very same power of the Spirit which brought about the mighty resurrection of the crucified Christ is at work in the fellowship of believers (Eph. 1:19-23). The congregation grows as the Spirit empowers disciples to bear clear witness to the Lord Jesus Christ, from Jerusalem to Judea, from Samaria to the uttermost part of the earth (Acts 1:8; 2:47). By the strength of the Spirit, the Church is purified and perfected (II Thess. 2:13).

It is the Spirit who represents the Head of the Church. Indwelling the worshiping fellowship, He calls and appoints men to be overseers of the flock of God redeemed by the blood of His beloved Son (Acts 20:28). The Spirit qualifies elders and deacons for their service in the household of faith. They edify the people of God only as they show themselves to be men "full of the Spirit and wisdom" (Acts 6:3). Evangelists and missionaries are summoned by the Spirit to cross cultural as well as national and linguistic barriers in presenting Christ. (Acts 13:1-3). And it is the Spirit who gives efficacy to their words and deeds so that sinners are converted, saints confirmed, and Christ glorified. Without the indwelling Spirit, it would be a mission impossible. Because of Him, the gospel gets to people "not simply with words, but also with power, with the Holy Spirit and with deep conviction" (I Thess. 1:5). The humbling and yet encouraging truth is that "unless the Spirit opens the minds and hearts of the hearers, as well as the mouth of the preacher, there can be no real communication of the gospel".[10]

In the seventeenth century, Paul Gerhardt wrote a hymn praying for the presence of the Spirit within the fellowship of the Church. Its closing verse asks,

> Come, Thou best of all donations
>   God can give, or we implore;
> Having Thy sweet consolations
>   We need wish for nothing more.
> Come with unction and with power,
>   On our souls Thy graces shower;
>   Author of the new creation,
>   Make our hearts Thy habitation.[11]

This prayer is echoed by the final stanza of another familiar hymn of the Holy Spirit:

> Spirit of purity and grace,
>   Our weakness, pitying see:
> O make our hearts Thy dwelling place,
>   And worthier Thee.[12]

Saying or singing these prayers, however, is never enough. We must actually open ourselves to the presence and power of Christ so that we are surrendered to His lordship and know the indwelling of His Spirit. How can the doctrine we profess lead us to experience the power we desire?

First, we must believe that the Spirit of God and the power He brings are as available to us today as to the people of God in

---

10. Ibid, p. 120.

11. Paul Gerhardt, hymn, "Holy Ghost, Dispel our Sadness."

12. Harriet Auber, hymn, "Our Blest Redeemer."

the past. Second, we ought to ask God for the fulfillment of His promise. It is only by asking do we receive, seeking do we find, knocking do we see doors opened to us. "God loves us, and wants to get to us more than we want to get to Him. We reach out to Him in every way we know. And we shall begin to find Him reaching out to us".[13] Third, we have the responsibility to part with whatever hinders us from receiving God's gift. This means giving up doubt, envy, jealousy, greed, pride, lust, laziness, anger, or anything else that stands in the way. Fourth, we should definitely decide to act on what God offers in His gospel, and act with obedient trust in His Word. These four steps should be helpful to churches and individuals eager to experience Christ within.

The Church today needs reformation and revival. These necessities will become realities as we come to commitment and not simply because we appoint committees. Yielded to the lordship of Christ, we experience the presence and power of the Spirit that will ultimately edify, unify and sanctify us. Indwelt and filled with the Spirit, we know the joy of fellowship. By Him possessed, directed, and empowered, we will serve one another in love and witness to Christ in the world.

The truth is that "When the Church has power, the world gets intrigued. When the Church has power, the world gets convicted. When the Church has power, the world gets converted ... What the Church truly needs is the Holy Spirit, deep fellowship at the center of its life, and witness in life and words as its overflow".[14]

PREPARING HIS HABITATION

The presence of God in the life of man and the fellowship of His people is often described by the witness of Holy Scripture in terms of indwelling. The Bible also speaks of sin as lodging

13. Samuel S. Shoemaker, *With The Holy Spirit And With Fire* (New York: Harper & Brothers, 1960) p. 38.

14. Ibid, p. 96.

in the depths of human personality (Rom. 7:17), and describes ungodly Babylon as a home for demons and evil spirits (Rev. 18:2). Far more frequently, however, it dwells on the promise and reality of the Divine indwelling.

In the Old Testament, mention is made of heaven as God's holy habitation. But this great God of purity and glory desires to dwell in the midst of His people. The tabernacle and the temple were places where God would manifest His presence to Israel. That is why pious Israelites went reverently and joyfully to the house of God, and loved the site where His glory dwelt (II Chron. 29:6; Psa. 26:8; 122:1).

In the Old Testament, God revealed His willingness to indwell the individual. Speaking for Him, the prophet Isaiah declared: "For thus saith the high and lofty One that inhabiteth eternity, whose name is Holy; I dwell in the high and holy place, with him also that is of a contrite, and humble spirit, to revise the spirit of the humble, and to revive the heart of the contrite ones." (57:15, KJV).

It is in the New Testament that the truth of God's indwelling within the church and the individual believer is fully revealed. Paul's writings abound in such references. Here are some of them:

Rom. 8:9-11, the Spirit of God dwells in the life of the disciple now, and will raise up the believer's body from the dust of death.

Eph. 3:17, Christ dwells in our hearts by faith.

Col. 3:16, the word of Christ dwells richly in the heart of the Christian.

I Cor. 3:16, the Spirit of God who lives in the individual disciple also inhabits the fellowship of the church and makes it God's holy temple (Eph. 2:20-22).

II Cor. 6:16, God wants to dwell in the midst of His people, and we may know His presence as we steer clear of idolatry and immorality in the determination to serve Him alone.

John 14:21, 23, The Father and the Son will take up residence in the lives of those who love Christ and demonstrate the sincerity of that affection in genuine obedience.

The Father and the Son come to dwell within us as we become the habitation of the Holy Spirit. That is what Pentecost is all about—Christ present, powerfully present within the lives of His people, for service and witness in the world.

How shall we preach the message of Pentecost and prepare the human heart to be His habitation? Clear preaching on this theme is a great need today. The charismatic movement has called renewed attention to the person and work of the Holy Spirit. Incidentally, the term, *charismatic*, as generally used, is a misnomer. Rather than be applied exclusively to those who say they have the gifts of tongues, interpretation, or healing, it belongs to all who have received any gift or charisma from God. Every Christian, having received the gift of the Spirit, is a charismatic in the biblical sense of the word (Rom. 8:9; I Cor. 12:13).

There are two extreme positions which must be isolated in any discussion of the subject and rejected. The first one is that anyone who claims to have spoken "in tongues" is psychologically defective or demonically possessed. The godly zeal of Pentecostalists in world evangelization, particularly in Latin America, should be sufficient to explode that prejudice. The second view is that anyone who does not practice glossolalia is deprived of the fullness of the Spirit and should, therefore, be considered a second-class member of the kingdom until he does. Both Scripture and experience run contrary to this view as well as the other.

The fact that there is a charismatic controversy animating and agitating much of contemporary Christianity should not turn us aside from the plain proclamation of the truth on the basis of what is revealed in Holy Scripture. God's written revelation, rather than man's prejudices or feelings, must be our authority in the matter of the Spirit no less than in that of doctrine dealing with the Father and the Son.

Indeed, we ought not to separate the Spirit from the Father and the Son. He is sent to us by the Father and the Son, and

His work is to bring us back to the Father through the Son. He leads us to Christ, cleanses us of our sin, and glorifies the Lord Jesus as our Saviour and King. Christ dwells within us by His Spirit.

It is most appropriate that the message of Christ within be presented after the remembrance of His redemption at Calvary, resurrection from the dead, and exaltation to the place of power and authority at God's right hand.

Following Easter and Ascension, we come to the day and season of Pentecost. The ancient Jewish festival of that name commemorated the giving of the law to Israel in the time of Moses, and the first-fruits of the harvest with gratitude to the God of providence. Ever since the memorable outpouring of the Spirit in fulfillment of the promise given through Joel (Acts 2:14-21; Joel 2:28-32), Pentecost has marked the descent of the Spirit of Christ and His indwelling within us.

A sermon series expounding a group of chapters in John's gospel would be very appropriate in this connection since they contain several promises of our Lord concerning the coming of the Spirit:

14:16, 17 — In answer to the prayer and merits of the Son, the Father will give the disciples another Counselor/Comforter to guide, strengthen and encourage them. This personal representative of the Lord Jesus Christ is the Spirit of truth, sent to be with them forever. He lives with the disciples and will dwell in them.

14:18, 19 — The disciples will not be left comfortless or orphaned in the world. Christ will come to them again after His passion and death, not only in resurrection glory but especially through the descent of the Spirit. Because He lives, they too shall live. This means more than the resurrection of the body at the last day, referring to the vitality now experienced by those whom the Spirit of life indwells.

14:25, 26 — The Counselor, the Holy Spirit, whom the Father will send in Christ's name, will teach the disciples all things and remind them of what Christ has said. This assures us of an accurate gospel record from the pen of those thus guided, and encourages us to believe that the Spirit will continue to keep our faith's focus on Christ.

15:26, 27 — The Spirit of truth, sent by Christ and proceeding from the Father, will testify to Christ. Our testimony in evangelism is strengthened and made effective as the Spirit creates conviction and brings illumination in the hearts and minds of those to whom we witness regarding His person and work.

16:12-14 — The Spirit of truth promised by Christ will come to guide us into all truth. And what is truth? God's Word is truth (John 17:17). The Spirit gives us insight as the meaning of God's Word, incarnate in Christ and inscripturated in the Bible.

Consider a careful presentation of the first two chapters of the Book of Acts for the season of Pentecost:

1:1-3, where we have a prologue for Theophilus, containing information about the production and purpose of Holy Scripture, and an indication concerning the meaning of discipleship.

1:4-8, in which the activity of a true God's witness is described as to sphere, strategy, and strength.

1:9-11, presenting the ascent of Christ (retrospect), and the return of Christ (prospect).

1:12-14, see the disciples devoted to prayer in a close fellowship, awaiting the promise of the Spirit.

1:15-26, the choice of the thirteenth apostle, made necessary by the defection of Judas, requiring the selection of one who had encountered the risen Lord and would share with the other apostles in making Him known.

2:1-13, the presence of the Spirit, descending to the accompaniment of transient but significant sights and sounds.

2:14-21, the promise of the Father, mistaken as intoxication, but fulfilled as predicted by inspiration, and resulting in the invocation of the name of the saving Lord.

2:22-36, the presentation of the Messiah, concentrating on His ministry, death, resurrection, and enthronement.

2:37-41, the progress of the gospel, produced by conviction, furthered by counsel, and issuing in commitment.

2:42-47, the prosperity of the church, characterized by perseverance, reverence, benevolence, and confidence.

Bearing in mind our Lord's promises to the witnessing disciples and what the Scriptures teach about the work of the Spirit in the process of salvation, you should plan to present a sequence of sermons dealing with New Testament conversions. In this connection, you will find James Buchanan's book "The Office and Work of the Holy Spirit" very useful. He details the Spirit's ministry in the conversion of sinners and their subsequent sanctification, as well as comments on revivals of religion.

Another Pentecost season might see the presentation of Christ within by the powerful presence of the Spirit as portrayed in chapter eight of the Roman epistle:

8:1-4, note that to be in Christ Jesus means experiencing liberation from the sequence of sin and death by the operation of the Spirit of life; also, that the redeeming work of Christ for us is related to the sanctifying work of the Spirit of Christ in us.

8:5-8, see the contrast between the attitudes and actions of the sinful man, and those of the spiritual person — one who is indwelt by the Spirit, thinks of what the Spirit desires, submits to God's law, and experiences life and peace.

8:9-11, where we are told that the same Spirit who raised up Christ will resurrect the Christian's body from the grave, and even now works in the soul to mortify sin and quicken obedience to righteousness.

8:12-17, filled with teaching on what it means to be a child of God: led by the Spirit; free from servile, guilty dread; confident in approaching a loving Father; heirs of God's riches; related to Christ in His sufferings as well as His glory.

8:18-25, present sufferings will be followed by the revelation of glory; we wait for the fullness of the glorious freedom of God's children, and the resurrection of the body, sustained by the Spirit who is already at work within us.

8:26-27, the Spirit helps us in our weakness, encouraging us to pray, enlightening us as to priorities for prayer; praying for us in accordance with the will of God.

8:28-39, a portion of Scripture rich with references to the sovereign grace of God and the mediatorial work of Christ, although the Spirit is not expressly mentioned, it is precisely such biblical material that He brings home to our hearts (as Christ promised) to guide, strengthen, and sanctify us.

The Galatian epistle puts a great deal of emphasis on the purity of the gospel of grace. It stresses reliance on Christ and His redemption as sufficient for salvation, apart from any idea of human merit or righteousness acquired through the performance of rituals or good works. It also reveals many truths about the works of the Spirit who represents Christ within us. The Spirit is given to those who believe the gospel (3:1-5). The Spirit assures those whom Christ has redeemed regarding their relationship to the Father (4:4-7). The Spirit enables us to use our gospel freedom to fulfill God's law by enabling us to crucify rather than gratify the desires of our sinful nature, and producing in us the fruit of love, joy, peace, patience, kindness, goodness, faithfulness, gentleness and self-control (5:13-26).

In Ephesians we find many passages descriptive of the presence and power of the Spirit. Here are some of them:

1:11-14, we were chosen in Christ, predestined according to the plan of the sovereign God, so that we might trust in Christ and live for His glory; hearing the word of truth, responding to the gospel of salvation, we were marked with the seal of the Spirit who guarantees our inheritance of all that God has promised His people.

1:15-23, a prayer in which reference is made to the Spirit who raised up Christ as the very One who now works mightily in the lives of believers.

2:19-22, converted Gentiles, like Jews who have found their Messiah in Jesus, belong to the one true people of God; they are living stones in a temple built on the prophetic-apostolic foundation, with Christ Jesus as the chief cornerstone; together, they are a holy temple in the Lord, a dwelling in which God lives by His Spirit.

The Spirit figures in the creation of Christian unity and the attainment of real maturity (Eph. 4:1-16). Active in the process of sanctification, in which we die to sin and live to righteousness, He must be treated with reverence and honored with obedience (Eph. 4:17-32). The fullness of the Spirit shows itself in a new quality of life marked by communication, praise, thanksgiving, and mutual submission (Eph. 5:18-21). The implications of that submission for our family life and economic existence are clearly spelled out by the apostle (Eph. 5:22-6:9). Our warfare with the powers of darkness, moreover, can only be fought and won as we use the sword of the Spirit, which is the Word of God, and remember to pray in the power of the Spirit (Eph. 6:10-20).

The expositition of I Corinthians 12-14 is also most appropriate in the season of Pentecost. We need the reminder of authentic, authoritative biblical revelation concerning the use and abuse of spiritual gifts. These are given by the sovereign Spirit for the edification of the body of Christ, not the gratification of the individual ego. Only as gifts are exercised in love do they build up the Christian community and further the witness of the church in the world to the glory of God.

It is both interesting and informative to consider the role of the Spirit in the life of Jesus Christ and discover the analogy between His activity in Christ and in the Christian. Think, for example, of the miraculous conception. Jesus was conceived of the Holy Ghost and born of the Virgin Mary without human paternity. Our rebirth by the power of the Holy Spirit, without the methodology or might of men, is a parallel to that miracle (Matt. 1:18-25; John 3:3-8; 1:13). As the descent of the dove at the baptism of Jesus accompanied the voice of the Father who assured Him of a unique sonship, so the Spirit bears witness in our hearts and assures us of our adoption into the family of God (Matt. 3:16, 17; Rom. 8:14-16; Gal. 4:4-7). The temptation, ministry, death, and resurrection of Jesus Christ also show the presence of the Spirit in His life and provide analogies for an understanding of the Spirit's work in our lives.[15]

To experience the meaning of Christ within us is no unhealthy mysticism but the very essence of true spirituality. It is the indispensable condition of vital Christianity and is made possible by the indwelling of His Spirit in our hearts. The truth is that "God is not only above us as a demand, He is within us as a source, a source of living water . . . springing up unto eter-

---

15. Mariano Di Gangi, *The Spirit of Christ* (Grand Rapids: Baker Book House, 1975).

nal life"[16] By the Spirit who comes to reside and preside in our hearts, the risen Lord comes to us with "all His regenerating, sanctifying, sealing, and comforting influences"[17]

What is true of the individual disciple is also true of the Christian community. We may know the presence of the absent Lord among us when we gather in His name, with ears to hear what His Spirit is saying as He speaks in the Scriptures. The exalted priestly king enthroned above continues to fulfill a prophetic ministry in our midst by His Word and Spirit. Surely this should give us a strong incentive to study biblical revelation and proclaim the whole counsel of God when His people meet for worship.

Christ has, moreover, promised to go with us into all the world, to the end of time, for the accomplishment of mission. He does this by the indwelling power of His Spirit and in infallible direction of His Word. "The missionaries of the gospel never go forth alone; where they go, the Presence goes also." Let us realize that "the Person who has ascended to heaven and sits on the right hand of God, exercising all authority in heaven and on earth, is Himself with the Church or her solitary representative in the most distant or hostile of heathen lands ... the Lord's 'I am with you' holds good so long as the world lasts for all who give their lives to the carrying out of His great commission"[18]

Hymns on the theme of the indwelling Christ and the presence of the Spirit are most appropriate, not only when preaching on some of the passages mentioned during the season of Pentecost, but before the reading or preaching of the Word in any service of worship. Rather than the well-intentioned but misguided cacophony of a group whose amplification drowns out any message their song might have conveyed, have the congregation sing a hymn of the Spirit as a proper preparation for the hearing of the Word.

---

16. Claudel, *I Believe*, p. 166.

17. Winslow, *Holy Spirit*, p. 88.

18. H. B. Swete, *The Ascended Christ* (London: Macmillan, 1910) pp. 125, 126.

Among the hymns that come to mind are "Spirit Divine, Attend our Prayers," "Come, Holy Ghost, our Souls Inspire," "Spirit of God, Descend upon My Heart," "Our Blest Redeemer, ere He Breathed His Tender Last Farewell," "Breathe on Me, Breath of God," "O Breath of Life, Come Sweeping Through Us," "Holy Ghost, Dispel Our Sadness," and "Come, Dearest Lord, Descend and Dwell."

Particularly related to the work of the Spirit in the inspiration of the Scriptures and illumination of its readers are hymns like, "The Spirit Breathes upon the Word, and Brings the Truth to Sight," "Father of Mercies, in Thy Word what Endless Glory Shines," "Lord, Thy Word Abideth," and "O Word of God Incarnate."

On the theme of union with Christ and His indwelling by means of the Spirit and the Word, we think of such hymns as "I've Found a Friend," "Christ, of All My Hopes the Ground," "Jesus, Thy Blood and Righteousness," "O Jesus, I Have Promised to Serve Thee to the End," "Jesus Where'er Thy People Meet," "Have Thine Own Way, Lord," and "Loved with Everlasting Love."

Discern whether or not a hymn faithfully presents Christian truth wedded to a harmonious tune and discard whatever is deadly ponderous or merely sentimental. Discover scriptural praise selections still buried in your own hymnal or waiting to be found in the hymnals of other churches. Introduce them tactfully. It is better to have new hymns introduced by the choir using them as "anthems" in the course of worship services, rather than to spring them on an unsuspecting congregation comfortably enjoying its liturgical rut. Or, if your church is numbered among the remnant that still has a midweek meeting, why not try a new hymn there before introducing it in a Sunday service of worship?

Let the harmony of message and music, preached from the pulpit and sung by the people, aim at the conversion of the uncommitted and the confirmation of disciples, to the glory of our Triune God.

Epilogue

"In the presence of God and of Christ Jesus, who will judge the living and the dead, and in view of his appearing and his kingdom, I give you this charge: Preach the Word; be prepared in season and out of season; correct, rebuke and encourage — with great patience and careful instruction. For the time will come when men will not put up with sound doctrine. Instead, to suit their own desires, they will gather around them a great number of teachers to say what their itching ears want to hear. They will turn their ears away from the truth, and turn aside to myths. But you, keep your head in all situations, endure hardship, do the work of an evangelist, discharge all the duties of your ministry. For I am already being poured out like a drink offering, and the time has come for my departure. I have fought the good fight, I have finished the race, I have kept the faith. Now there is in store for me the crown of righteousness, which the Lord, the righteous Judge, will award to me on that day—and not only to me, but also to all who have longed for his appearing" (II Tim. 4:1-8).

These are the words of a man about to be martyred for his unwavering commitment to the cause of Christ. They constitute a clear call to all whom the Lord entrusts with ministry. Let us listen to what the Spirit is saying in this Scripture.

EXHORTATION

In a series of crisp imperatives, we hear a most stirring summons to Christian service. The Spirit who inspired the apostle's words does not offer suggestions. He issues orders. And these definite demands are put in a most solemn setting: in the presence of God, and of Christ Jesus, who will judge the living and the dead, and in view of His appearing and kingdom (II Tim. 4:1).

Christ Jesus shall judge all men of every time and place. Those who are still alive on earth at the moment of His advent shall certainly not evade that encounter. And the dead shall arise to be confronted with the One who has been appointed of God to execute judgment. Surely the thought of that day should stimulate us to faithful service in these remaining days. To the returning Christ must we then render an account of our negligence, obedience, or disobedience.

Our Lord will appear in all His royal majesty when He comes again. We shall see this King resplendent with heavenly glory. The Spirit, through this Scripture, points us forward to "His coming, at which we shall stand before Him; His kingdom, in which we hope to reign with Him".[1]

Let us, therefore, live in the light of what has been prophesied. May we never lose sight of "the great realities of the future world, which should infinitely outweigh all the present: Christ's appearing, when everything in the past shall be

---

1. Henry Alford, *The Greek Testament,* revised E.F. Harrison, 4 vols. (Reprint, Chicago: Moody Press, 1958), III:398 (on II Tim. 4:1).

brought into judgment; and His kingdom, when His faithful servants shall reign with Him in glory".[2]

The apostolic charge is crystal clear. Paul's challenge is to "Preach the Word" (II Tim. 4:2). Note the primacy of preaching. Paul does not say, "Administer the organization." He doesn't urge, "Raise the funds." He doesn't plead, "Hold a healing campaign." He says, "Preach!"

Don't misunderstand the apostle. He is not saying that administration is unimportant. Remember his insistence on the recruitment and training of suitable elders and deacons to whom aspects of congregational life may be delegated. Nor is he saying that money doesn't matter. Paul praises the Macedonians for their generosity in supporting his missionary service, gathering funds for famine relief, and gives much teaching on the stewardship of our material blessings. Nor is the apostle saying that we should be unconcerned with the alleviation or cure of disease and deformity through the means God has provided. What Paul is saying, however, is that preaching must be honored with primacy in Christian ministry.

The fact is that preaching is held in rather low esteem by many professing Christians today. At least some of the blame must fall on the preachers themselves. The man who proceeds to preach without the required preparation of heart and mind, treating both the Word and people of God with contempt, brings preaching into disrepute. So does the minister who turns the pulpit into a forum for the parading of his own doubts, or the airing of prejudices, or the imposition of legalism on understandably restive hearers. And what of those men who abuse the privilege of preaching by engaging in the amateur practice of psychology, or who pretend to be experts in politics and economics instead of proclaiming the God-appointed message?

Congregations are not guiltless in the matter of contributing to the depreciation of preaching. If they refuse to recognize the

---

2. Patrick Fairbairn, *Commentary on the Pastoral Epistles.* 1874, (Reprint, Grand Rapids: Zondervan, 1956), pp. 382, 383 (on II Tim. 4:1).

pastor's need for adequate time to study the Scriptures and prepare sermons, they betray a view of the ministry that falls short of what is plainly presented in the New Testament itself. Many members, moreover, are becoming increasingly restive. They resent being told anything by anybody in an authoritative way. Discussion? Yes. Declaration through preaching? No.

It is my firm conviction that one of the greatest needs of the churches in our time is the recovery of reverent biblical exposition and the relevant application of truth to personal, family, and societal problems. The recovery of real preaching in the power of the Holy Spirit will make for the renewal of Christianity today.

In his incomparable allegory *Pilgrim's Progress*, John Bunyan portrays a serious soul whom Christian meets in the house of the Interpreter. His eyes are lifted to heaven, the best of books is in his hand, the law of truth is written on his lips, and the world is behind his back. Does Bunyan's description fit the contemporary cleric?

"Preach." You are an authentic, authorized herald of the King. Your commission is not to invent a message, but to deliver it faithfully. Don't subtract from it whatever may not pass through the filters of the sceptical mind in order to make the message acceptable. Don't add to it the cultural accretions and arbitrary legalisms that would please men but pollute the message. Deliver what God has entrusted to you. Preach. Like John the Baptist, you must prepare the way for the Way by serving as a voice crying in the wilderness of this morally barren world. Crying? Surely not whimpering. The word, as used by the gospel writers with reference to John, conveys the sound of a bellowing bull or a roaring lion. Lift up your voice. Lift it up with strength. Be not afraid, apologetic, or ashamed. Preach!

"Preach the Word." This is the message—the Word of God. Make known through preaching what God has revealed in His Word. This means expounding and applying the supernatural revelation given through human instrumentality by the inspiration of the Holy Spirit in the Holy Scriptures. "The Bible is the Word *par excellence* . . . the one authorized record of the workings of divine Love in meeting our sin and death . . . the only Book on earth which carries upon it the imprimatur of the Son of God as the authentic revelation of Himself".[3]

Preach the written Word, both the law which condemns sin and the gospel whose focus is on the Saviour; both the precepts expressive of God's demands, and the promises indicative of His grace; both faith extended to receive forgiveness, and works motivated by gratitude for mercy; both our duty in this present world, and our destiny in the world to come. Preach the Word revealed and preserved in the Holy Scriptures.

Preach the incarnate Word, Jesus Christ. Present His deity and humanity. Declare and apply His messianic offices as the infallible prophet, merciful priest, and righteous king. Proclaim His humiliation and rejoice in His exaltation. Preach the incarnate Word from the written Word.

Preach the Word, conscious of God's call to do so. Understand that He "will have His truth preached by the mouth of men; therefore, He hath appointed the ministration of His Word that we might know His will; for God useth this means, that men may know His truth." The plain fact is that "God hath shut up His truth in the Scriptures, and will have it preached and expounded to us." Again, "How shall we know Him unless we allow ourselves to be taught by His Word?" Let us "reverence the doctrine of the Word of God" for "God will have His truth maintained by means of preaching".[4]

Preach the Word in season and out of season. Look for opportunities to present Christ from the Scriptures. Apply God's truth to human needs, ever speaking that truth in love. Your ministry will require correction, rebuke, and encouragement. Correct—make your appeal to reason on the basis of divine

3. H.C.G. Moule, *The Second Epistle to Timothy* (London: The Religious Tract Society, 1905) p. 127 (on II Tim. 4:2).

4. John Calvin, *The Mystery of Godliness* (Reprint, Grand Rapids: Eerdmans, 1950) pp. 116, 119, 120, 121.

revelation, challenging people to see and to do what is right. Rebuke — especially when moral discipline is deplorably relaxed, appealing to the conscience, desiring the reclamation of the erring. Encourage — addressing the will, and putting new heart into your hearers so that they act on the call of God to confidence in Christ, repentance for sin, and obedience to the Lord.

Encountering indifference and hostility, our corrections and rebukes may tend to become harsh and irritating. Thus the apostle urges that we fulfill our pastoral ministry "with great patience" (II Tim. 4:2). The same word needs to be told to parents as well as pastors.

At all times let there be "careful instruction" (II Tim. 4:2). If we would see people involved in the practice of what is good, then we must give them good principles through sound, careful teaching. The doing of the truth is dependent on the teaching of the truth. Duty should be related to doctrine. That master teacher, Calvin, reminds us that "reproofs either fall through their own violence or vanish into smoke, if they do not rest on doctrine".[5] Let us, then, keep exposition and application together. The former, divorced from the latter, becomes pedestrian and irrelevant. The latter, separated from the former, is bereft of authenticity and authority.

EXPLANATION

Why this insistent, urgent call to *"Preach the Word?"* Why the need to engage earnestly in a ministry requiring correction, rebuke, and encouragement? The answer is found in this sad prediction: "For the time will come when men will not put up with sound doctrine" (II Tim. 4:3). They will choose entertainment rather than education, so that the church loses its in-

5. John Calvin, *Commentaries on the Epistles to Timothy, Titus, and Philemon*, trans. William Pringle (Edinburgh: Calvin Translation Society, 1856) p. 253 (on II Tim. 4:2).

tended character as the school of Christ. They will regard the teaching of the prophetic/apostolic message, with its doctrines and duties, as an intolerable yoke. Jaded with the truths of redemption and resistant to the ethics of regeneration, they will look for something else and find it.

Instead of feeding on sound doctrine, people are following religious propagandists who confirm their prejudices and gratify their whims. Fascinated by fads, hungry for the sensational and swallowing both superstition and speculation, they show no spiritual discernment. Their interest is in "something newer, more mysterious, more alluring to curiosity, than the gospel of the Crucified and the dutiful path of holiness".[6]

So they turn from the truth and follow mere myths. Charlatans exploit their religious sensibilities. Sects and heresies take them in, and they are drawn into the vortex of personality cults. They may even be lured by the occult. Because they will not listen to the truth, God will justly let them be misled by a lie.

In view of this dreadful drift and deviation from sound doctrine in favor of falsehood, the servant of Christ must renew his commitment and fulfill his ministry. As Calvin comments, "The more grievous the diseases are, the more earnestly Timothy should labour to cure them; the nearer dangers are at hand, the more diligently he should keep watch".[7]

"Keep your head in all situations" (II Tim. 4:5). Be awake, alert and aware to what is going on. With presence of mind, use every opportunity to speak and act the truth. Clearsighted, discern the temptations of the devil who would depress, divide, distract, delude, and defile. Recognize his tactics, and resist him firmly. Keep your sense of balance. Act without overreacting. Show real sobriety and moral sanity in a world gone

---

6. Moule, *Epistle*, p. 131 (on II Tim. 4:3).

7. Calvin, *Commentaries on the Epistles to Timothy, Titus, and Philemon*, p. 257 (on II Tim. 4:5).

mad with lies. Evaluate everything in the light of the eternal
realities revealed by the Spirit in the Scriptures.

"Endure hardship" (II Tim. 4:5). In this world, you shall have
tribulation. Don't expect universal applause and unfailing ac-
claim. Be ready to endure affliction in the course of obedience.
Show a steady spirit, bearing up under pressure, overcoming
the temptation to quit, neither shrinking from difficulties nor
shirking duties, but continuing with high courage in His cause.

"Do the work of an evangelist" (II Tim. 4:5). But what is "an
evangelist?" Look afresh at "Philip the evangelist" (Acts 21:8).
See him preaching the Word in the Samaritan city. Hear him
presenting Christ as the Suffering Servant of the Lord, sacrificed for the sins of His people on the basis of the inspired
Scriptures. Behold him leading others to saving faith in Jesus,
the Son of God, and understand what "the work of an
evangelist" really is (Acts 8:4-8; 26-40).

The pastor must feed the flock of God. He is called to edify
believers and further the development of their discipleship
through biblical teaching and understanding counsel. Yet the
task to which God summons you involves far more than caring
for the ninety and nine sheep safely in the fold. It also requires
a quest for the one lost sheep. It includes evangelism no less
than edification. "Do the work of an evangelist," and encourage
other Christians to share your concern in this enterprise of
love.

"Discharge all the duties of your ministry" (II Tim. 4:5). For
the good of the individual, the growth of the church, and the
glory of God, give adequate attention to every aspect of your
ministry. Render a complete and effective service. This doesn't
mean that you are expected to excel in everything—preaching,
visiting, counseling, administering, teaching, and evangelizing.
But it does involve the fulfillment of a balanced ministry free
from the blight of exaggerated emphasis on some things and a
tragic neglect of others.

Note that Timothy is challenged "to accomplish his sacred
task, to perform all its functions, to accept all its duties, to

realize all its possibilities, to be faithful to all its demands".[8] We need to hear and obey this challenge in our day, since the risk of failure regarding some vital aspect of the Christian ministry is very real.

A scholarly pastor may spend a great deal of time preparing sermons in his study, but may fail to find time to visit the sick and comfort the bereaved. An out-going minister may devote himself to visitation and small fellowship groups and then give the remaining, waning energies of his mind to sermon preparation at the close of a busy week. Let us be careful to show a sense of balance in the fulfillment of our ministry.

EXPECTATION

The apostle stands in the lengthening shadows of mortality and martyrdom. He considers the present, reviews the past, and contemplates the future with clear perception.

Paul considers the present. He knows that he is already being "poured out" on the altar (II Tim. 4:6). The life that Paul has presented to God in living sacrifice is now approaching the moment of death. Here is a man who is truly surrendered to his Lord, loving Him with heart, soul, mind, and strength. That is why he has no dread of dying. Paul is also aware of the fact that his "time for departure" has come (II Tim. 4:6). Like a ship loosed from its moorings for that final journey, the apostle knows himself to be homeward bound. Soon he will be absent from the body, but present with the Lord.

Now Paul reviews the past: "I have fought the good fight, I have finished the race, I have kept the faith" (II Tim. 4:7). The apostle "did not fear death, because he had the testimony of his conscience that by the grace of God he had in some measure answered the ends of living".[9]

---

8. C.R. Erdman, *The Pastoral Epistles of Paul* (Philadelphia: The Westminster Press, 1923) p. 120 (on II Tim. 4:5).

9. Matthew Henry, *An Exposition of the Old and New Testament*, 9 vols. (London: Nisbet, 1857) IX: 487 (on II Tim. 4:7).

As a loyal soldier of Jesus Christ, the apostle had fought the good fight with magnificent courage, undaunted by obstacles and opposition. The race had been long and difficult. No short sprint, but a course demanding discipline and drive to reach the goal. The faith entrusted to him has been faithfully kept. Here is a man of unquestioned doctrinal integrity who has refused to barter away the great truths of our historic Christian faith for a mess of rationalist pottage.

Paul views his life for Christ in retrospect. "The days and nights of care and toil, the fight with temptations outward and inward, the conflict with subtle and aggressive error, 'the thorn in the flesh, the messenger of Satan,' the extreme physical exhaustion amid the personal perils and half-deaths of those long travellings — it is a finished story".[10]

And what is the prospect? The man who has lived for Christ has the blessed assurance that the best is yet to be. After the life of service, involving struggle, suffering, and even sacrifice, there will be a sequel of glory. The crown awaits the conquest. The Lord who promises a crown of life to those who are faithful unto death, and holds out a crown of unfading glory to hearts of pastoral concern, will award the apostle a "crown of righteousness" at the last day (II Tim. 4:8; Rev. 2:10; I Peter 5:4). In this world, the Lord's people may be treated with shameful injustice. But when "the righteous Judge" returns, their faithfulness and love shall not fail to be recognized and crowned by Him.

Will the crown of righteousness be reserved exclusively for martyred apostles? Not at all. It is offered to "all who have longed for his appearing" (II Tim. 4:8).

We live between the two appearings or epiphanies of our Lord. The first advent was one of grace, in which He was revealed as the Redeemer who liberated His people from the penalty and power of sin. At His second coming, He will be revealed as the King of glory (Tit. 2:11-14). As the writer of the

---

10. Moule, *Epistle*, p. 143 (on II Tim. 4:7).

letter to the Hebrews puts it, "He has appeared once for all at the end of the ages to do away with sin by the sacrifice of himself . . . Christ was sacrificed once to take away the sins of many people; and he will appear a second time, not to bear sin, but to bring salvation to those who are waiting for him" (9:26, 28).

To long for His appearing not only expresses faith, "but such a full assurance of faith and hope in Him as casts out fear, and comes with the confidence that when He appears, we shall also appear with Him in glory".[11] On the other hand, "all who are so much devoted to the world, and who love so much this fleeting life, as not to care about the coming of Christ, and not to be moved by any desire of it, deprive themselves of immortal glory".[12]

His glorious appearing is our blessed hope. We long to be with Him and share in His triumph over death, our last enemy. We look forward to beholding Him, and yearn to be transformed into His likeness. We love His appearing because we love Him who first loved us.

We have the promise of His coming. Jesus says, "I am coming soon." And our longing hearts respond, "Amen. Come, Lord Jesus." (Rev. 22:20).

---

11. Fairbairn, *Pastoral Epistles*, p. 393 (on II Tim. 4:8).

12. Calvin, *Commentaries on the Epistles to Timothy, Titus, and Philemon*, p. 263 (on II Tim. 4:8).

Bibliography

PROLOGUE

Blackwood, A.W., *Planning a Year's Pulpit Work*.
  New York: Abingdon Press, 1942.

Calvin, John, *The Deity of Christ and Other
  Sermons*. Grand Rapids: Eerdmans, 1950.

Clowney, E.P., *Preaching and Biblical Theology*.
  Grand Rapids: Eerdmans, 1961.

Cunningham, William, *Historical Theology*. 2 vols.
  (1862). Reprint. London: Banner of Truth Trust, 1960.

Daniel-Rops, *Jesus and His Times*.
  New York: E.P. Dutton, 1954.

Di Gangi, Mariano, *The Spirit of Christ*.
  Grand Rapids: Baker Book Hosue, 1975.

Edersheim, Alfred, *Life and Times of Jesus the Messiah*.
  2 vols. New York: Longmans, Green, 1900.

Gibson, G.M., *The Story of the Christian Year,*
New York: Abingdon Press, 1945.

Guthrie, Donald, *Jesus the Messiah.*
Grand Rapids: Zondervan, 1972.

Harrison, E.F. (edit.), *Baker's Dictionary of Theology.*
Grand Rapids: Baker Book House, 1960.

Hengstenberg, E.W., *The Christology of the Old Testament.*
4 vols. Edinburgh: T. & T. Clark, 1858.

Henry, C.F.H. (edit.), *Basic Christian Doctrines.*
New York: Holt, Rinehart & Winston, 1962.
(edit.), *Jesus of Nazareth: Saviour and Lord.*
Grand Rapids: Eerdmans, 1966.

Luther's *Meditations on the Gospels.* (arranged by
R.H. Bainton. Philadelphia: Westminster Press, 1962.

Macartney, Clarence E., *Twelve Questions about Christ.*
New York: F.H. Revell, 1923.

Rochelle, Jay C., *The Revolutionary Year.*
Philadelphia: Fortress Press, 1973.

Schaff, Philip (compiler), *The Creeds of Christendom.*
3 vols. New York: Harper & Brothers, 1877.

Sheen, Fulton J., *Life of Christ.*
New York: McGraw-Hill, 1958.

Smith, David, *The Days of His Flesh,*
London: Hodder & Stoughton, 1910.

Stewart, James S., *A Faith to Proclaim,*
London: Hodder & Stoughton, 1952.

Torrance, T.F., *When Christ Comes and Comes Again.*
Grand Rapids: Eerdmans, 1957.

Williams, J.G., *The Church Year Makes Sense.*
London: SCM Press, 1963.

CHRIST WITH US

Berkouwer, G. C., *The Person of Christ.*
Grand Rapids: Eerdmans, 1964.

Boettner, Lorraine, *The Person of Christ.*
    Grand Rapids: Eerdmans, 1943.
Liddon, H.P., *Advent in St. Paul's*
    London: Longmans, Green, 1889.
    Christmastide in St. Paul's.
    London: Longmans, Green, 1890.
Machen, J. Gresham, *The Virgin Birth of Christ.*
    New York: Harper & Brothers, 1930.
McDonald, H.D., *Jesus: Human and Divine.*
    Grand Rapids: Zondervan, 1968.
Morris, Leon, *The Lord from Heaven.*
    Grand Rapids: Eerdmans, 1958.
    The Story of the Christ Child.
    Grand Rapids: Eerdmans, 1960.
Smith, Wilbur M. (compiler), *Great Sermons on the Birth of Christ.* Natick, Mass.; W.A. Wilde, 1963.
Warfield, B.B., *The Person and Work of Christ.*
    Philadelphia: Presbyterian & Reformed, 1950.
Westcott, B.F., *The Incarnation and Common Life.*
    London: Macmillan, 1893.
    The Revelation of the Father.
    London: Macmillan, 1894.

CHRIST FOR US

Babbage, S.B., *The Light of the Cross.*
    Grand Rapids: Zondervan, 1966.
Berkouwer, G.C., *The Work of Christ.*
    Grand Rapids, Eerdmans, 1965.
Denney, James, *The Death of Christ.*
    London: Hodder & Stoughton, 1902.
Hodge, A.A., *The Atonement.*
    Philadelphia: Presbyterian Board of Publication, 1867.
Hoeksema, Herman, *The Amazing Cross.*
    Grand Rapids: Eerdmans, 1944.
Krummacher, F.W., *The Suffering Savior.*
    Reprint. Grand Rapids: Baker, 1977.

Liddon, H.P., *Passiontide Sermons.*
London: Longmans, Green, 1891.

Loane, Marcus, *Life Through the Cross.*
Grand Rapids: Zondervan, 1966.

Martin, Hugh, *The Shadow of the Cross* (1875).
Reprint. Glasgow: Adshead & Son, 1955.

Morris, Leon, *The Apostolic Preaching of the Cross.*
Grand Rapids: Eerdmans, 1955.
The Cross in the New Testament.
Grand Rapids: Eerdmans, 1965.
The Story of the Cross.
Grand Rapids: Eerdmans, 1957.

Pink, A.W., *The Seven Sayings of the Saviour on the Cross.*
Swengel: Bible Truth Depot. 1919.

Sangster, W.E., *They Met at Calvary.*
New York: Abingdon Press, 1956.

Schilder, Klass, *Christ in His Suffering.*
Grand Rapids: Eerdmans, 1942.
Christ on Trial, 1945.
Christ Crucified, 1940.

Smeaton, George, The Apostles' Doctrine of the Atonement
(1870). Reprint. Grand Rapids: Zondervan, 1957.
*The Doctrine of the Atonement as Taught by Christ
Himself* (1871). Reprint. Grand Rapids: Zondervan, 1953.

Smith, Wilbur M., (compiler), *Great Sermons on the Death of
Christ.* Natick, Mass.: W.A. Wilde, 1965.

Young, E.J., *Isaiah 53.*
Grand Rapids: Eerdmans, 1952.

Zwemer, Samuel, *The Glory of the Cross.*
London: Oliphants, 1954.

CHRIST OVER US

Berkouwer, G.C., *The Return of Christ.*
Grand Rapids: Eerdmans, 1972.

Bosc, Jean, *The Kingly Office of Christ.*
London: Oliver & Boyd, 1959.

Denney, James, *Studies in Theology.*
London: Hodder & Stoughton, 1898.

Green, Michael, *Man Alive.*
Chicago: Intervarsity Fellowship, 1967.

Liddon, H.P., *Easter in St. Paul's.*
London: Longmans, Green, 1890.

Maclaren, Alexander, *After The Resurrection.*
New York: American Tract Society (no date).

Martin, James, *Did Jesus Rise From the Dead?.*
London: Lutterworth Press, 1956.

Milligan, William, *The Ascension and Heavenly Priesthood of our Lord.* London: Macmillan, 1894.
The Resurrection of our Lord.
London: Macmillan, 1894.

Orr, James, *The Resurrection of Jesus.*
London: Hodder & Stoughton, 1908.

Pache, Rene, *The Return of Jesus Christ.*
Chicago: Moody Press, 1955.

Smith, Wilbur M. (compiler) *Great Sermons on the Resurrection of Christ.* Natick, Mass., W.A. Wilde, 1964.

Swete, H.B., *The Appearances of our Lord after the Passion.*
London: Macmillian, 1908.
The Ascended Lord.
London: Macmillan, 1910.

CHRIST WITHIN US

Buchanan, James, *The Office and Work of the Holy Spirit* (1843). Reprint. London: Banner of Truth Trust, 1966.

Candlish, James S., *The Work of the Holy Spirit.*
Edinburgh: T. & T. Clark, 1886.

Green, Michael, *I Believe in the Holy Spirit.*
Grand Rapids: Eerdmans, 1975.

Howard, David M., *By the Power of the Spirit.*
Downers Grove, Ill.: Intervarsity, 1973.

Kuyper, Abraham, *The Work of the Holy Spirit* (1900).
Reprint. Grand Rapids: Eerdmans, 1941.

Morgan, James, *The Scripture Testimony to the Holy Spirit.*
Edinburgh: T. & T. Clark, 1865.

Morris, Leon, *Spirit of the Living God.*
Chicago: Intervarsity, 1960.

Moule, H.C.G., *Veni Creator.*
London: Hodder & Stoughton, 1892.

Owen, John, *A Discourse Concerning the Holy Spirit* (1674).
Reprint. London: Banner of Truth Trust, 1966.

Shoemaker, S.M., *With the Holy Spirit and with Fire.*
New York: Harper & Brothers, 1960.

Smeaton, George, *The Doctrine of the Holy Spirit* (1882).
Reprint. London: Banner of Truth Trust, 1958.

Stott, J.R.W., *The Baptism and Fullness of the Holy Spirit.*
Chicago: Intervarsity Fellowship, 1964.

Thomas, W.H.G., *The Holy Spirit of God.*
Chicago: Institute Colportage Association, 1913.

Winslow, Octavius, *The Work of the Holy Spirit* (1843).
Reprint. London: Banner of Truth Trust, 1961.

EPILOGUE

Adams, Jay, *Pulpit Speech.*
Philadelphia: Presbyterian & Reformed, 1974.

Blackwood, A.W., *Expository Preaching for Today* (1943).
Reprint. Grand Rapids: Baker Book House, 1975.
Doctrinal Preaching for Today (1956).
Reprint. Grand Rapids: Baker Book House, 1975.
Preaching from the Bible.
New York: Abingdon Press, 1941

Davis, H. Grady, *Design for Preaching.*
Philadelphia: Fortress Press, 1958.

Dillistone, F.W., *Christianity and Communication.*
New York: Charles Scribner's Sons, 1956.

Lloyd-Jones, D.M. *Preachers and Preaching.*
Grand Rapids: Zondervan, 1971.

Marcel, Pierre, *The Relevance of Preaching.*
Grand Rapids: Baker Book House, 1963.

Macpherson, Ian, *The Burden of the Lord.*
New York: Abingdon Press, 1955.

Miller, Donald G., *Fire in Thy Mouth.*
New York: Abingdon Press, 1954.

Morgan, G. Campbell, *Preaching.*
London: Marshall, Morgan & Scott, 1937.

Nichols, Sue, *Words on Target.*
Richmond: John Knox Press, 1963.

Reindorp, George, *Putting It Over.*
London: Hodder & Stoughton, 1961.

Stalker, James, *The Preacher and His Models.*
London: Hodder & Stoughton, 1891.

Stewart, J.S., *Heralds of God.*
London: Hodder & Stoughton, 1946.

Stibbs, A.M. *Expounding God's Word.*
London: Intervarsity Fellowship, 1960.
Understanding God's Word.
London: Intervarsity Fellowship, 1950.

Stott, J.R.W., *The Preacher's Portrait.*
London: Tyndale Press, 1961.

Taylor, William, *The Ministry of the Word* (1876).
Reprint. Grand Rapids: Baker Book House, 1975.

Warren, Max, *The Day of the Preacher.*
London: A.R. Mowbray & Co., 1967.

White, R.E.O., *A Guide to Preaching.*
Grand Rapids: Eerdmans, 1973.

Yohn, D.W., *The Contemporary Preacher and His Task.*
Grand Rapids: Eerdmans, 1969.